THROUGH THE FIERY FURNACE

THROUGH THE FIERY FURNACE

DAVID MAENDEL

authorHOUSE®

AuthorHouse™
1663 Liberty Drive
Bloomington, IN 47403
www.authorhouse.com
Phone: 1-800-839-8640
© 2011 by David Maendel. All rights reserved.

First published by AuthorHouse   06/29/2011

ISBN: 978-1-4634-2903-4 (sc)
ISBN: 978-1-4634-2902-7 (dj)
ISBN: 978-1-4634-2901-0 (ebk)

Library of Congress Control Number: 2011911269

Printed in the United States of America

Back Cover Photo (Siege Ramp at Masada) by David Maendel

This is the story of my life and the things that have happened to me in 64 years. Butit must be remembered that what is written here in this manuscript is entirely from memory. I believe that my memory is fairly accurate. But it is entirely possible that some inaccuracies may have occurred. It is not my intent to bring harm in any way too anyone from any inaccuracies that may have occurred. There is nothing written in this book that is in any way intended to be malicious, harmful, or insulting intentionally. All of the names in this manuscript have been changed with the purpose of protecting everyone involved. I do not accept any responsibility for any deviation that may have occurred from actual facts of occurring incidences that are written about in this manuscript. This manuscript has been written to the best of my knowledge. But is done entirely from memory and this must be taken into consideration when this manuscript is read.

Dedication

There are so many people in my life I could dedicate this book to. There are people who have been very helpful to me along the way. Some of these people have paid a high price to help me. Some of them have paid with their very lives. However the proper dedication for the book must go to three very distinct individuals. I dedicate this book first of all to God the Father. The one who oversees all things, prepares all things, sets all things in motion, and prepares all things in creation with total perfection. The one who knows all things before creation ever happened. God Almighty who is the perfect supreme power in all of creation. The one from whom all power emanates, has its purpose, and the one to whom all power and authority in the universe must answer to. Without God's purpose and perfect plan I would not be here. I find so very fascinating the minute details that the Lord God has taken time to set in place. Every detail no matter how minute serves a very important purpose in God's plan. It is also very important to understand that the enemy in all his attempts to destroy or derail us from our God-given purpose never succeeds. It is also important to understand that God Almighty has no plan A or plan B. This is because God's planned A is always perfect and without flaw.

I also dedicate this book to a man who was born in Bethlehem and a humble stable. Born of a virgin over 2000 years ago. The man Jesus who is the Christ the anointed Messiah of God. He has paid the highest price for me, a price that I could never pay myself. With the shedding of his blood on a cruel wooden cross he bought my soul and spirit unto eternal salvation. His death sealed my salvation for all eternity. No power in creation can take this very special gift away from me. This is the finest and most precious gift that anyone could ever give to us. But his work did not end there. By the stripes that he bore my heeling is made complete 2000 years ago. In seven places the Lord Jesus shed his blood and broke every curse that has ever been levied against the human race. He gave us a doctrine and the new covenant that was sealed in his blood. If we follow his plan that is laid down in the New Testament there is no power in creation that can prevent us from achieving the gift of eternal life. His work was not finished yet. After he died on the cross he was placed in a borrowed tomb. On the third day the stone that covered the entrance to this borrowed tomb was rolled away. Jesus Christ our King walked out of the tomb for he had risen from the dead.The healing hand of the Lord Jesus has been extended to myself and my family on so many different occasions. A lot of these occasions have been written in this manuscript. Because of the transforming power of Jesus shed blood on the cross and because of the transforming power of baptism by submersion in water and because of the transforming power of the baptism of the Holy Spirit I am able to walk whare God is taking me. Without these three vital elements I would never be able to serve my God the way he has asked me to. Because Jesus Christ has accompanied me on all of my walk since the moment I was conceived he has empowered me by his presence in me to overcome every single obstacle that has ever been thrown in my way. As Jesus himself told me on two different occasions,"I have never left you and I will never leave you. You will never be without my presence in your life. You have only to call on my name to secure my help. I have given you all of the weapons you need to fight the deceiver every time he attacks you. You have all the necessary tools that you will need to go where I am taking you. If you will follow me and believed in me and allow me to build your faith I will guide you to where I want you." This has always been true in every situation and circumstance in my life.

I also want to dedicate this book to the Holy Spirit whose presence is always with me. He has filled me with his presence and has led me into the rest of God. When I first entered into the rest of God I was quite confused and did not understand what had just happened to me. Learning to live in the rest of God took me considerable time to get used to. The first and most important thing that I noticed about living in the rest of God was the peace and joy that is so overwhelmingly present at all times. No matter what happened in my life from that point on I was always filled with peace and joy. The Holy Spirit has brought me understanding of God's word. He has brought me understanding of God's purpose. He has brought me understanding to a large degree of who and what God really is. The Holy Spirit on many occasions has brought me tremendous revelation of things that are yet to come. Some of these things I can speak about with other people others I cannot yet speak about to anyone. The Holy Spirit has guided me in everything that I have ever done. He has caused me to be totally and completely dedicated to what the Lord is doing with me. The Holy Spirit has caused me to be completely and totally uncompromising in the understanding and revelation that he has given me of the word of God. All of my life the Holy Spirit has been my guide. Everything that the Lord Jesus has asked me to do the Holy Spirit has guided me to complete every task. Without the presence of the Holy Spirit in my being my life would have almost no meaning. He has become my true friend and companion.

I also want to dedicate this book to my two children who are the love my life. My son Jeremy told me one time not too many years ago"dad I've been listening to you talk about the work that you are going to perform for the Lord in Israel as long as I can remember." I think that sometimes my son has thaught me to be a little bit unbalanced. But Jeremy has always believed in me. He has also helped me in many ways in the talents and gifting that God has given him to use. Jeremy also is alive because of the instant healing touch of the Lord Jesus in an emergency. Jeremy in many ways has also been a tremendous inspiration and encouragement to me in the writing of this book. Jeremy has also been there to keep telling me that there are times when I need to back off and wait for the Lord to move.

I would also like to dedicate this book to my daughter Melissa. Melissa has brought me such a tremendous amount of joy that it is difficult to describe. After my experience with the cult and learning how to hate, it was my daughter Melissa who was very instrumental in teaching me how to love again. From the moment that she was born she has always been filled with the natural love of God. She has never let me forget that I am her dad and that she loves me without compromise. Melissa has truly been a treasure to me and the wonderful gift from the Lord. She has also been very faithful and her devotion to her father in spite of a lot of nasty things that she has heard about me.

To both of my children Jeremy and Melissa I want to say thank you so much for being who you are and for your support and love and companionship you have given me in this life. I also know that we will have eternity to spend discussing the details that we missed in this life. You are both the love of my life second only to the God that I serve. I know there is coming a time when I will have to leave and you will not be able to see or hear from me for quite a while. But cheer up because we will see each other on the other side. My prayer for both of you is that you will always stay faithful to the Lord. Learn also always to praise and thank him for where you are and for the healing hand that he is extending to you. Without the healing hand of God you would both have died as little children. You are both always the cherished treasure of my life.

Chapter 1

The Lord Has a Purpose

Since I was 20 or 22 years old I have wanted to sit down and put into wordthestory of my life. But I wanted to do this so that it would bring glory to God.Because I've really felt for many years like Paul says in the word, that the life I live now I do not live but Christ lives through me.If Christ lives my lifethrough me, I stillhave a right to tell the story of my life. But that story should be told in a way thatbringsglory and honor to Christ and the Holy Spirit and Jehovah, God of my people. I was told by the Holy Spirit that I am of Jewish descent, of thetribe of Judah. So the story that I tell is a story of a man who had very humble beginnings. I guess it's difficult for me to tell the story because in so many ways it is going to seem as though I am bragging a lot. I would like to make clear that this is not my intent. If I brag, my brag is about my heavenly Father and about the might andpower of the Lord Jesus, and about the in failing presence of the Holy Spirit.From thetime I was born I was different than all of the people around. I was different to the point of being considered an oddity. Condemned by many of my relatives as well as people in the community that were not related tome. I was also an easy target for persecution by other people. This always seems to be the case with people that are call to service by Jehovah. The enemy always maligns people who serve God in a powerful way. But at every turn tries to derail us, or destroy us. I've lived a life of almost constant persecution.The persecution did not have only one source it was directed at me through many different people in many different situations and almost all the time.In every bit of persecution that I suffered the Holy Spirit always protected me.In every bit of persecution or trial that came against me Jehovah wanted me to learn something. I discovered at a fairly young age that if I paid close attention to God's leading me and pay attention to the persecution and trial that I was undergoing at the time, I could learn the lesson that was intended for me to learn and there by being led out of the persecution or trial quicker. I stayed in the trial or persecution the longest when I concentrated on other people that were being used by the enemy to persecute me. If forgiveness was in my spirit the trial past a lot more quickly, the protection of the Lord was much more prominent throughout the persecution. It is my intent in this book to tell the story about my life. Just as important to tell of the characteristics, the grace and mercy, the unending love and the healing hand of the Lord God. You have to understand I came up the hard way. There was never anything easy about my life.All of the trials, tribulations, persecutions and hardships that I have suffered have done a very good job of developing me to be the kind of vessel that God can use for a specific purpose. God always develops us for a specific purpose. The trials and persecution that we are allowed to go through in the process of our training, are therefore specifically designed to prepare us for specific service. That is why my persecution and tribulation and suffering are never the same as anyone else's. As the word of God says we are all members of the same body. We are all filled with the same Holy Spirit. We are all a part of the same body. But are all different parts of that body.We are allused in different ways. But if we allow the fullness of the indwelling presence of the Holy Spirit to work in us and through us then God is glorified in all that we do. We must at all times maintain a forgiving, loving spirit. I think that the most difficult part of my training was to forgive the people who were responsible for the damage caused to my family and for the personal damage caused to me. After the Lord asked me to forgive he also asked me to lay down the burden of pain that I had been carrying all of my life. Laying down the burden of pain was more difficult than the forgiveness. It seems like the pain we bear in our spirit to a large degree is our identity. When we laid down at burden of pain it is like we are laying down a part of who we are. This is very difficult to do but extremely necessary. Coming out from under the yoke and bondage of unforgiveness and carrying around the burden of pain releases us to serve God. It clears our spirit so that God through the Holy Spirit can fill our spirit with his presence.

With unforgiveness in our spirit we cannot hear the voice of God speaking to us through our spirit. We have to free ourselves from all bondage and come out from under everything that the enemy burdens us with. We have to learn to let go of every hold and every method the enemy uses to detain us or blind us or keep us from hearing the voice of the Holy Spirit.

Chapter 2

The Beginning

Where I grew up in North Dakota was a small valley that dropped some 200 feet
below the tabletopflat land that surrounded it. If you've ever driven through that part of the country you will know that it is as flat as a tabletop. The little valley where we made our home was actually a river valley. A small stream flowed through one side of this valley. The valley was some 3500 feet across and it was large enough to build a small community. The Christian group that we lived with bought this place in 1949 or 1950. My family moved to this place in the summer of 1950. My father with the help of other men in the community started the construction of our home as soon as we arrived. The first part of bulding the housewe lived in, was to dig a hole in the ground that was some 10 feet deep and about 8 feet in diameter. This hole was lined with concrete and served as a dry well to catch and collect water off the roof. This was our primary water supply for the house. The house that we lived in was moved to that location as a complete unit. This house was actually at one time an old icehouse. The walls in his house were some 8 inches thick. So the house was extremely well insulated. The installation in this house made a big difference in being able to heat in winter. We heat our homes at that time primarily with wood. The only running water we had in this house was a hand pump that drew water out of the drive well. The only electric in this house was one of electric light in the living room. There was no indoor plumbing. For bathroom facilities we used an outhouse that was located about 75 or 100 feet in back of our house. For bathing we used a large wooden washtub in the middle of the living room floor or we went swimming in the river and got ourselves washed

that way. The men who were preparing this house for us to live in had finished digging the hole for the dry well. My sister Rachel was carrying my brother Solomon when she came to close to the edge of the dry well and fell into it carrying Solomon in her arms. Solomon did not get hurt, but Rachel my sister broke her elbow. This event seemed to christen our home. When the cistern was finished, the house we were living in was moved over top of the dry well. The Maendel House was not a large house it was about 30 feet long and 25 feet wide the first floor consisted of the entryway, the living room, and the master bedroom. The stairway that led to the second floor was on one side of the living room. The upstairs consisted of two bedrooms. The front bedroom of the house was my sisters Rachel and Barbara bedroom and the back bedroom of the house is where Ben and John and I slept. I am the oldest boy of a family of 14 children. Five girls and nine boys made up our families. There seem to have been a small controversy when I was born. The controversy was over what my name should be. Traditionally in a Hutterite family the oldest girl is named after the mother. The oldest boy is named after the father. My father's name is David, so naturally my father would name me David as well. But my father wanted to break with that tradition. However an argument with my mother convinced my father that he had no choice. But my father did not name me after himself but rather he named me after King David of the Bible. This was done without saying a word to my mother at the time. At the time he never explained to her why he had named me David. By the time my mother discovered that I had not been named after my father I was four or five years old. This upset my mother to the degree that she almost considered me not one of the family. From this point forward I was for sure not my mother's favorite child. At the time I was born my mother really wanted another daughter.

I was born at home in our house in Portage la Prairie Manitoba Canada. I was delivered by my grandmother. The day before I was born bad weather sets into that part of Manitoba Canada. The temperature dropped to 20° below zero. A blizzard started to blow and dropped visibility to almost nothing. This blizzard continued to blow for 2 ½ days. When my grandmother delivered me, the top drawer of my father's dresser was taken out and the contents of socks and underwear were removed. A baby blanket was placed in the drawer and I was put into the drawer. This became my cradle until I was almost a year old. I guess the purpose of this method was so when I cried and made too much noise the drawer was placed back into the dresser and was closed. My mother always treated me as some kind of an outsider.

When I was still only about two years old and running around outside in the yard there were a number of times when my mother lost track of me. The first few times this happened a search party was formed to look for me. But every time I was finally found I was with my father. After a few times of this happening my mother just waited until my father came home from work and I was always with him.

The house where I was born in new Rosedale colony was a fairly small house. I distinctly remember that the siding of this house was composed of imitation brick.This material was composed of beaverboard that had been impregnated with tar. I also remember the large wood stove that stood in the living room off to one side.

A small creek had carved a ravine through one side of this community. In order to cross this raven the men of the community had installed a swinging bridge. This swinging bridge was anchored to trees on one side of the ravine and to steel poles driven into the ground on the other side of the ravine. Just plain boards had been put down on the bottom cables of the swinging bridge to serve as a walkway. By watching my father I figured out how to cross the swinging bridge. One day when I was less than four years old while following my father I crossed the swinging bridge. However I only got halfway across when other older boys caught me in the middle of the bridge. These older boys went to swinging this bridge back and forth. The only recourse that I had was to lie flat on my belly and hang onto both sides of the bridge. At this point I started to yelling as loud as I could and my dad heard me and came back and rescued. All I saw was myself in the bottom of the ravine which was about 25 or 30 feet deep. I don't believe my father let these two little boys forget that swinging his son on this bridge was a bad idea.

Chapter 3

Father Was Everything

My father's job at New Rosedale was to raise geese and turkeys from day-old chicks until they were finally sold at nine months old. My father was also responsible for the commercial incubators to hatch out the chicks.

I was always very fascinated with the process of hatching these checks out in it large commercial incubators. It was amazing to me to see the chicks pack holes in the eggs from the inside so that they could escape from the eggshell. The baby geese were quite easy to start. All we had to do was place them in pens with water and feed and they knew enough to eat the food and drink the water. Baby turkeys on the other hand are not that smart. Turkeys when they are first hatched out of the egg must be taken one at a time and manually dipped their beaks into water and then into the food. Then only do they know enough to drink water and eat food to survive.

At this point in the life of these young birds there is still a great deal of work to be done in order to ensure their growth to be healthy adults. Temperatures in the surrounding pens must be monitored regularly. They also have to be very closely checked for disease. I always remember being with my father when he was working and when I was not in school.

My relationship with my father was very close. My father had two daughters and finally the third child was his son. I was my father's pride and joy. And my father to me was the best thing that ever happened since the invention of fire. I would rather be with my father in his daily work than anywhere else doing anything else. I don't think there's anything else that I would rather have done than to be with my dad. But in the community my dad was always an underdog. And when it came to disputes between him and someone else the treatment that my dad received greatly wounded me.

In wintertime when my dad was not raising geese and turkeys my dad was a shoemaker. My dad made all the shoes for everyone in the colony. The small building that my dad used as a shoe shop was always comfortably warm in winter. It was a magnificent place to go for us kids when we got cold.Five or six or seven of us would get into his shoe shop and hang around the stove to warm up. But when my dad had had enough of kids being in a shoe shop he opened the wood stove and put in a piece of rubber tire. The increased heat very quickly drove all the kids out of a shoe shop. I never remember my dad ever asking any children to leave the shoe shop. This was his method of eviction and it was quite efficient.

I remember my dad being a craftsman at whatever he was doing. All of my dad's work was done to perfection at all times.He always gave far more than he was required. My dad was talented and gifted at everything that he did. Whether he was making shoes carving animals out of a piece of wood with a penknife or making furniture. My dad was a craftsman. He took considerable pride in the fact that he did his work well and beyond criticism. So when somebody came up to my dad and unjustly criticized him for his work or the way he conducted himself it wounded me deeply. Because I knew that my dad was not like that.

My early childhood I remember as being the happiest time of my life. My early years especially the time I spent with my dad to me were the sweetest years of my childhood. I think one of the problems I had in my relationship with my mother was that she never knew where I was. Because a great deal of that time was spent with my dad. To say that I idolized my dad I realize is a strong term but I guess I reverence him. I truly looked up to him and I wanted to be obedient to him in everything that he told me to do. The reason I wanted to be obedient to my dad in everything had a lot less to do with the punishment for disobedience than it did for the respect and reverence I had for my father.

I remember vaguely an incident that happened while we were still living in Canada. It was still early summer and my dad had already started to raise turkeys. The turkeys were old enough to be turned loose on the range of course in a penned in area. I followed my dead one morning when I was about two and half years old. He went down to the turkey pan to check on the young birds. He opened the gate and walked through it and held it open for me to follow. As I followed him into the turkey pen a few turkeys started following me. When I looked behind me and saw a number of turkeys following me I started to walk a little faster. The problem with turkeys is when they see somebody new they follow him. The faster I walked to get away from the turkeys the more turkeys followed. The more turkeys that followed me the faster I walked. This cycle grew until over half the flock of turkeys was following me. By this time however the turkeys were no longer following they were chasing me. Again my dad had to come to my rescue.

I believe it was in the summer of 1950 when it was our families turn to move from Portage la Prairie Manitoba Canada to Force River colony in Fordvilll North Dakota. The move from Canada was a very exciting time for me. We were on our way to a brand-new home. Along with the new home came an altogether new life. Although our life in North Dakota was basically the same from day to day the surroundings were entirely new and different. At the time of this move I was about four years old. Getting to explore my new surroundings with the other boys and girls my age was going to be incredibly exciting

Chapter 4

The New Colony

The buildings that house the families of the community were located at the southern end of this valley. The church, which also served as the school, was located in the southwestern corner. In the far northwestern corner of this valley was located the pig farm. Just to the south of the pig farm was located the laying chickens. It was just to the south of the chicken barns that the large commercial incubators were located in a small building. From the chicken barns directly east some 500 yards was located the repair garages. In the northeast corner of the valley was located the dairy barns. A hundred yards east of the dairy barns the river ran along the eastern edge of the valley. It was along the edge of this river 100 yards south of the dairy barns where my dad keeps the turkeys and geese.

Along the edge of the river where the geese and turkeys were my dad constructed a large waterwheel. The water wheel was designed to pick up water and dump it into a trough that carried the water for the geese and turkeys.

This river that entered the valley in the far northwest corner and ran east and then turn to run south along the eastern edge of the valley. This river was less than 20 feet wide at the widest spot and the deepest spot in the river was not more than 2 ½ or 3 feet deep. At the farthest northwest corner the men of the colony dug out an area in the river large enough and deep enough for swimming hole. This area in the river also served as a very good place to cut ice out off in the winter. Cutting blocks of ice in winter was an important activity in the community. The ice was stored by the cow barn and covered with sawdust and sand to preserve it. In summer June and July and August the ice was dug up and used to make ice cream.

This practice started years before when ice was used in coolers and freezers. We never quite give up that practice of cutting ice.

Forest River colony was mixed farming. We had a pig farm, layingchickens; we also raise chickens for food for ourselves. Then we had dairy cows, we also had beef cows. We raised geese and turkeys mostly for sale commercially. Most of the beef cows that we raised were either sold as young calves or as year old stock. The laying chickens provide eggs for our own use as well as for sale to supermarkets in Grand Forks. The pig farm was primarily for the sale of pigs. But this also provided us with pork products. On this farm we also raised our own sheep. A lot of the woolfrom the sheep was processed into yarn for use in knitting sweaters, socks, and mittens, hats, and long johns. I don't know very many people anymore who can say that as they grew up they worelong johns made out of sheep's wool. Wool long johns are the warmest I have ever worn. But in order to wear these you have to find a way to get past the itch. But the sweaters, Socks mittens, and hats were incredibly wonderful to wear in winter. My mother and sisters knitted all of these for us.

On the farm we also planted and raised all of the grain products wheat,barley, oats, corn as well as alfalfa and other hay. We also planted a large vegetable garden. Vegetables for our own use and for canning.

I think that about all we bought in town was material to make our clothing out of and sugar and salt. We also purchased leather and other material for shoe. Everything else that we needed we raised on the farm. The women made all the clothing that we wore. My dad was a shoemaker and made all the shoes that we wore. All of our food supplies were raised on a farm. We ground our own cornmeal as well as our own flower. Our fresh water supply came from a spring that flowed out of the hillside in the far northwest corner of the valley. The water was pumped from the spring directly into large steel tanks. From these tanks the water was pumped to all of the residential houses as well as the barns. We also produced all of the grain and feed that we needed for our animals and livestock.

In the Southwest corner of the Valley and up on the Hill a grain elevator was built. This grain elevator served as a place to store some of our wheat, barley, and oats. It was also the place where we ground corn and other grains for cow and animal feed as well as corn and wheat for human consumption. In back of the grain elevator and to the south is where we kept the beef cows in winter. In summer the beef cows were out on a fenced off range where they could graze.From September until the end of May the children went to school that was located in our church.Anenglish schoolteacher was hired from outside the colony to come in and teach our children. We also had German school instruction. The same man that was our preacher taughtthis German school instruction to us. The language that we spoke in our everyday life was a dialect of Austrian. I really didn't speak any english until I was almost 8 years old. English was a very foreign language to me.

Our daily life at the colony was very well orchestrated and scheduled. Each one of the men had their own duties. One man's responsibility was the hog farm. Another man's responsibility was to care for the laying hens. Still another man took care of the dairy farm.Others were assigned to the beef cattle. My dad was assigned to care for geese and turkeys. He was also the one who ran the commercial incubators to hatch out young chicks young turkeys and young geese. In winter he spent his time making shoes for everyone in the community. He also spent a lot of time repairing shoes. Still others of the men in the community were assigned the responsibility of caring for the grain farm. They were also responsible for making sure that all of the hay and alfalfa was cut. Whatever duty the men were assigned to their sons worked right alongside of them.

Others of the men were assigned to the repair garage for the repair of equipment and machinery that was used on a continual basis on the farm. Another one of the men was assigned the responsibility as a carpenter. The carpet's responsibility was to do repairs in homes, built furniture, as well as construction of other buildings as needed. Whenever a large project was undertaken such as the building of a new building, the carpenter got all the help that he needed from other men.During the first part of the winter of 1950 I was hospitalized with double pneumonia. When my father took me to the hospital, the doctor informed him after I was examined that I would need to remain in the hospital. He also informed my father that I would likely not leave the hospital alive. Those doctors fully expected me to die of the pneumonia that I had. Because of the fact that my lungs were fully infected with pneumonia they did not expect me to live. I vaguely remember the second day my father came to see me becouse he brought me a six-pack of orange crush soda. When I could not drink it that day he asked the nurses to temporarily stored in the refrigerator. On the fourth day in the hospital, whenmy dad came to see me I walked out of the hospital with him. The Lord had miraculously healed me from an illness that should have killed me. For the six-pack of Orange crush soda that my father had brought me, the nurse's staff apologized to me for drinking it. They said they were sure that I was going to die therefore wouldn't need the soda. And the nurse's staff being diligent in their work hated to see the soda to go to waste.

During that winter of 1950 a great deal of time was spent by all of the men in the colony placing all the families in homes and making for sure that they were settled. Other work that they were required to do also had to be carried out as usual. The shoe repair shop building had been constructed behind the house we lived in.My father during the first winter was making and repairing shoes for a lot of the time. The other job that he was assigned to was that of incubating eggs for geese and turkeys. This job did not start untill the end of February 1951.

Chapter 5

Colony life

In a Hutterite colony everyone takes part in the work that needs to be done. However none of the people that actually work receive any money for their labor. Everyone is given the necessities of life. Someone that is assigned to be the financial manager, manages all the money in the colony. Church services in the colony were conducted every evening at six o'clock.Everyone in the colony was expected to be in church when church services were conducted. The only excuse that would get a man or a woman out of church on any given day was if their work required them to be somewhere else. On Sunday church services were conducted at 8 AM. And at 6 PM. The a.m. service let out at 11 or 11:30 AM. Evening services as a rule lasted an 1 ½ to 2 hours.

All life in the colony was strictly scriptural based. If a man or woman did not abide by rules and regulations set forth in Scripture, or rules and regulations that were established by the community they could be excommunicated. Excommunication consisted of an internal exile. They were not permitted to communicate with anyone or have any fellowship with anyone. This excommunication lasted untill they came in front of the church congregation and apologized for any wrongdoing that they were accused of, and forgiveness was granted to them. At that point they were reinstated as a full member of the colony. Excommunication very seldom occurred in a colony. The Hutterit colonies were very much a Pentecostal Christian group. One thing that they seriously objected to in the Christian life was the water baptism of children. Children in the Hutteritcolony were never baptized and were never dedicated. It is believed by the Hutterites that baptism should only take place when a child is old enough to understand the Scriptural reason for baptism.

They made every attempt to live their lives strictly according to Scripture.The Hutterites had their origin in 1428 in Europe at the time of the reformation. At that time the Catholic Church brought severe persecution against the Hutterites for refusing to join the Catholic Church. Many of our forefathers were tortured and killed for their faith. When the persecution got to be too harsh, as a group we fled into Austria. The King of Austria in the late 1400s and early 1500s granted the Hutterites a safe haven. When that safe havens ceased to be, and the Catholic Church continued their persecution, the Hutterites fled into Russia. In the late 1700s Canada needed settlers in the central part of the country. After hearing about the Hutterites, that they were farming people the government of Canada invited the Hutterites to immigrate to Canada. They were assisted in starting farms in the central part of the country. However 100 years later in the mid-to late 1800s the Hutterites owns so much land in the central part of Canada that the Canadian government was very much afraid that the Hutterites were capable of taking over the country. At this point they were encouraged to immigrate to the United States. By the 1920s Canada found itself again sparsely populated in the central part of the country. The Canadian government again invited Hutterites to come back to Canada and settle in the central part of the country. The Hutterites now own vast areas of land under farming. A small Hutterite colony consists of 50,000 acres. So if there is 100 colonies scattered out in Canadian Midwest they own a lot of land.The Canadian government in the late 1970s passed a new law that all families who made less than a certain dollar amount income, were eligible for welfare from the Canadian government. The Hutterites qualified for this government handout. However they chose not to receive it. But in order to convince a Canadian government not to send this money to them it was necessary for the Hutterites to file a lawsuit against the government. After successfully following through on this lawsuit the Canadian court handed down a ruling that the Hutterites were exempt from the government handout.To this day the Hutterites do not receive any government handouts of money for their survival. The governments both in Canada and the United States do not assist the Hutterites financially. The Hutterites are 100% self-sustaining and self-supporting. While the Hutterites use medical facilities in town, they always keep and care for their older people and anyone that may be mentally challenged.

In the Hutterites colony breakfast was always served at 6 AM. Lunch was always served at noon. Dinner was always served at 5 PM. Everyone there that wanted something to eat was required to be at these meals, which were served in the central dining room. A separate smaller dining room was for the young children up to age 16. 16 years and older were allowed to eat in the adult dining room. Anyone that missed a meal for no good reason was required to come back when the next meal was served. Life in the Hutterites was both simple and secure as long as you follow the rules.

Chapter 6

Father's Work

The Hutterites colony was also a very good place to grow up in as a child. There was always some new adventure to get involved with. There was always something to do. There was also always somewhere to get into trouble and most kids are pretty good at discovering that. As small boys my brothers and myself were always into something. Never anything drastically wrong, but always pushing the envelope. My father being a shoemaker never ran out of leather. He always had a strap hanging behind the doors of the house. And my father was not brutal in his discipline, but he did not like seeing his sons get into trouble. We were to exemplify to other children proper behavior. My father also did not want to be embarrassed by other people in the community coming to him and telling him how his sons had misbehaved themselves. If that scenario had ever happened, I am sure that it would have cost us extra stripes.

My father was very diligent in raising his children properly. Scriptural discipline was strictly enforced and used whenever necessary. But at the same time a lot of hours each day were applied towards instruction. This instruction happened while he was working and we were with him on his job, or at home. My father spent most evenings reading the Bible to his children. He would sit in his favorite chair and his children would gather around him sitting on the floor and he would read us Bible stories. Reading the Bible stories was only the beginning of instruction. We were expected to be able to hear and to relate the meaning of what we had heard. After the reading of the Bible stories there was always discussion. Dad did not always ask the most brilliant child for his opinion. A lot of times he picked on the younger ones to see what understanding they had acquired. And there was more time spent in giving the younger children more opportunity to understand Scripture so that they would not be left behind in any part of their understanding and education of the Bible. These times in the evenings when dad would gather the children around his chair to read Scripture to us where some of the most precious times that I can remember in growing up. It give us such a wonderful chance and opportunity to interact with each other as a family. Our interaction with each other was in the privacy of our own home. And there was no outside influence from other people. In the Hutterite community there still had to be individual family time. And the structure of a strong family was very much encouraged.

During the first winter at Forest River colony the Turkey and geese chicks that we were supposed to hatch in our own incubators we were unable to do. Because ofhigh startup costs of this farm the chicks were supplied by other colonies in Canada. We were required tomake regular trips to Canada to bring back the day-old birds. On a lot of these trips I was allowed to go with my father. While other of these trips men from the colony in Canada who delivered the young birds to us conducted. All that was required of us when we received the young birds was to start them. With the young turkeys this required taking each bird and dipping its beak into the water and then into the feed. The young geese were much easier to start. All we had to do was put them into the pens under the heat lamps with food and water and they start themselves. Once the young birds were started however they required 24 hours a day seven days a week care. The care of these young birds continued like this untill they had developed a good portion of their feathers. When the young geese and turkeys had grown old enough to grow a large portion of their feathers they required less prepared feed that was ground from grain that we grew. A larger portion of their feed was grass that we mowed along county roads from the ditches and roadsides. This also provided a service for the County so that the county people did not have to come out to mow the roadsides.

Because I was my father's eldest son I assisted him with all of this work. When I was five years old my dad taught me how to drive the tractor. It was necessary for someone to drive the tractor while my dad stayed in the back on a wagon to unload grass while I was driving through the geese pen.

My father kept very accurate records of his work with the young birds. He knew how many birds he started with, he also knew how many birds we lost in the season. He also kept track of how many bird'sraccoons, hawks, or other predators killed. At home my dad had a large oak desk of the old-fashioned variety. This desk had a roll top cover that pulled down and locked into place. Most of the time my dad did not bother to lock this desktop.

Chapter 7

Education Starts

In the summer of 1951 my dad acquired a new tape measure. This tape measure was a brand-new type the blade of which retracted because of a coiled up spring inside. When I was five years old this tape measure became an object of fascination for me. I was not satisfied with this tape measure snapping back in once the blade had been pulled out and released. I wanted to know what makes this tape measure go back in so fast. Actually what happened next was partially my father's fault? The tape measure was held together with one Phillips head screw in the center. But my father had left a Phillips head screwdriver lying in his desk right next to the tape measure. And being an inquisitive child continually searching the higher realms of knowledge to acquire a greater understanding of my surroundings, all I did was very carefully remove the Philips head screw from the center of the tape measure. I then very carefully pulled the two halves of the tape measure apart. No sooner had I pulled the two halves of the tape measure apart then all of the contents in the center jumped out at me. Now I had a real problem. How in the world am I ever going to get all of this thin steel back into that tiny case? No matter how hard I struggle to jam that stuff back into the case it just wouldn't fit. As I was home alone and there were no witnesses to my attempted gathering of vast quantities of knowledge through personal experience, I simply put the tape measure back into the desk and very carefully closed the roll top of the desk. I even made sure that the lock was secured. That evening when my father got home from working with a young geese and turkeys all day, he was quite tired. He sat down at his desk as he did every single day to make some notations in his record book concerning the young birds. He took a hold of the handle to the roll top desk and attempted to pull it up. He was quite puzzled when he discovered that the top had been locked. Because he never locked it. After unlocking the lock mechanism, he opens the top. When the contents of the compressed tape measure jumped out at him and almost hitting him in the face, he jumped straight up in the air in a sitting position with such a startled look on his face it had to be seen to be believed. When gravity finally took the better part of him and set him back down in his chair, he immediately yelled for me to present myself in front of him with my full-undivided attention. As you can imagine this was not a particularly joyful moment for me. I was well aware of the fact that my father was not about to compliment me on a job well done. But look at thing from the bright side. I did figure out how the tape measure worked, and what caused the blade to retract into the case so quickly. In order to acquire this knowledge anywhere other than the University of hard knocks would probably have cost me considerable amount of money. So the way I looked at it the practical experience was probably worth it. The bad side effect of all this was that it took my father well over an hour to wind the spring back up around the center core of the inside of the tape measure. I don't believe that my father was very happy with the way that the tape measure worked after this.

But my father was very forgiving provided I had learned a lesson. We had several discussions about this incident after this. He discovered during those discussions that I had indeed learned my lesson. But he also used some of the valuable leather that he had stripped off of the cowhide in belt size portions. And I did through this experience acquire a number of welts across my romp. But education is never inexpensive.

On some days there were a lot of hours when young boys were not really required to work with their dad. It was during these hours that we were required to find something useful to fill our time. Because of the number of men that were always around the colony there was never really any full-time supervision ascribed to us. So we found ways to entertain ourselves.One of the ways that we entertained ourselves was to go fishing. The small river was not very deep but on a good day we could catch enough fish to make a good dinner for two or four people. Another good way to stay busy that did a lot of good for people and provided nourishment at mealtimes, was to set snares to catch rabbits. We also found that if we caught rabbits especially around vegetable garden, that our vegetable garden didn't suffer as much damage. The rabbits that we caught with the snares were always cleaned and skin by us, which we learn how to do early, and taken up to the kitchen where the women in the kitchen always cooked them for us.My father, having by this time constructed a large waterwheel in the river, it required some care. It was our job when we were not busy doing other necessary chores to keep an eye on this waterwheel. The water was carried up by the waterwheel in cans and poured into a trough. When these cans came loose it was our responsibility to make sure they were reattached. It was also our responsibility to keep a watchful eye on the turkeys and geese to make sure that they had water to drink. Tom who was our schoolteacher for German school, gave us candy bars for every can full of nails and glass that we collected from around our property.

At the dairy barn, in a corral was where we kept a large Angus bull. This bull had a temper and we knew it. We used to love to go over teased the bull until he got mad at us. The corral was made up of railroad ties that had been sunk into the ground and a 2 x 6 fence nailed over these railroad ties. We got the bull mad enough he would charge at us while we were sitting on a split rail fence. But we would be sitting right by a railroad tie. And the bull would always hit his head into the railroad tie, which of course would not move very much. After a few times charging at the railroad tie like this the bull would become quite dizy and begin to stagger around. We also had a couple of horses in this corral and we would love to go over to feed the horses apples. But when we ran out of apples the only thing we had left to feed the horse was a red rubber ball about the size of an apple. We would give one of the horses this ball and a horse chew on the ball for about five or seven minutes. After chewing on red rubber ball for a period of time thehorse would finally spit the ball out. Animals were amazingly funny at times. And they were good source of amusement if they were contained in a safe spot.

The men from the colony had dug out a large enough hole in the river at the northwest corner of our property to serve as a swimming hole. After lunch was over on a lot of days in summer the children were allowed to go down to the swimming hole to swim for an hour. Again this was done primarily without supervision. But there were very often young people there who were as old as 12 or 14 years. We were quite fortunate that no mishaps ever occurred. When lunch got out it was always a race to the swimming hole to see who would get their first the boys or girls. Because we did not have swimming trunks we just took our clothes off and went in the water. So when the boys were swimming the girls were not allowed to be there. When the girls were swimming the boys were not allowed to be there.

Chapter 8

The Spirit Of God

And in summer just like in winter all the children were without excuse to attend church at six o'clock in the evening. We did not have any schooling in the summer. School generally was over by the end of May. School did not start again until October. But there was Sunday school every Sunday afternoon. All children in the community up to age 16 were expected to be there. The schoolmaster had a belt that he had acquired from my father shoe shop and he also knew how to use it. While his punishment was not brutal it was harsh. I always enjoyed Sunday school. I enjoyed learning about God and the things that the Lord had done for us. About our salvation by the blood of Jesus shed on the cross. I really enjoyed studying and learning about all of the people in the Bible. Our Sunday school was also very much enforced by my father at home. At home during the week we would go over our Sunday school lesson and the homework that we were given to do.My father madesure that we could memorize Scripture that we were given to memorize. Failure in memorizing Scripture was not an option. My father's children always remembered and could recite verbally all of their scripture without reading it from the Bible. Sunday school was always very strictly enforced at home and at school. Those children that thought they could get away without paying too much attention to Christian education in Sunday school always faced a leathery retribution. This is quite effective to get their attention in the future.

On one of these occasions I was the one that was singled out for punishment with his belt. Five stripes left five black and blue stripes on my back and buttocks. My brothers and I decided that we'd had enough of the belt. We stole the belt and threw it in the river.As we watched the belt floating down the river we forgot that it would float right past the schoolmaster's house.He just happened to be on the riverbank in back of his house fishing.Don't you suppose for a minute that he didn't catch the belt that floated right by him.While he didn't use the belt on the three of us as an educational means to keep us from stealing the belt in the future he promised that no further activity of this type would be tolerated.

The colony had hired an English schoolteacher from a nearby town. Our spoken language was a dialect of Austrian. We spoke Austrian all of our life. The colony provided this English schoolteacher so that we would have some instruction in the English language. We needed English in our life because we were always in town and had to communicate with secular society.This particular English schoolteacher was a young lady about 24 or 25 years old. The church is where school was conducted. The church was an old building that had been fixed up and remodeled and it had a tin roof. This one room building was heated with a wood stove. In early spring of one year we asked experienced some very severe weather. In the morning when we went to school there was still no sign of any storm. The clouds to the west could be seen becoming extremely dark. By 10 o'clock in the morning it had started to rain. The rain was very heavy at times and made considerable noise on the tin roof. Our english school teacher started to look quite anxious. The rain quite suddenly turned to hail. At first the hail made a light clattering noise on the tin roof. However when the hailstones got to be the size of tennis balls the noise was deafening. This hailstorm lasted for about a half hour. When it finally stopped all of the children looked around to see where the teacher was. We could not see her and we knew that she had not left. But we needed her permission to be excused so that we could go outside and look at the hailstones. We finally located our English schoolteacher under her desk. The hailstones that we found outside were truly the size of tennis balls. This hailstorm had done considerable damage on our crops. The crops however had just started to sprout. The damage at this point was not very severe.

Chapter 9

Ernie The Pig Man

Ernie was the man in the community that was in charge of taking care of the pigs. Up in the haymow of the pig barn was the place where we stored a lot of straw. Ernie developed a very good relationship with a man in Grand Forks who was the manager of a potato chip company. When he would go to Grand Forks on business, Ernie would take along a few dozen eggs, or some of our native honey or frozen geese to trade with this man in the potato chip factory for a 55-gallon steel drum full of potato chips. He would take the steel drum to the pig barn and hide it in the hey mow under the bales of straw. Whenever he had guests coming to his house he would always have a bunch of potato chips to give them. Nobody else in the colony had access to any potato chips. For a while it was a puzzle to us how Ernie was acquiring potato chips. The boys in the colony made it their business to watch Ernie very closely. It wasn't very long before guests came to his house and he wanted to serve them chips. We followed Ernie to the pig barn where we watched him go up into the hay mow and dig up the 55 gallon barrel of potato chips. The boys also like potato chips. After discovering where he had hidden the berrel, we dug it up ourselves and enjoyed helping ourselves to potato chips. Next time Ernie had guests to his house he made his usual trip to the barn to dig up his potato chip barrel to get potato chips. The only problem was the barrel is empty. Ernie new that just a few days before he had gotten a new barrel of potato chips so the barrel should have been full. After he discovered what had happened to the potato chips he tried very hard to find a new hiding place. The boys however always found where he had hidden the berrel. Ernie finally discovered that if he wanted potato chips for himself he had to make sure that the boys had some themselves to take home. Ernie discovered that with this method called sharing he was able to keep some for himself. Ernie was a hard man to educate with this trial and error method but after a while it seemed to work very well. The University of hard knocks always works well.Ernie was also a very hard man. He had little or no feeling in his entire being for animals. On occasion he would put together two male pigs that were full-grown. These two pigs would naturally fight. Each pig had tusks that grew out of its upper and lower jaw 2 to 3 inches long. When the fight was finally stopped the pigs were badly torn up. Ernie would use either to put the page to sleep so that he could stitch up their wounds. Causing these animals to fight like this and tear each other to pieces for no good reason drastically hurt my spirit and I stayed away from it after witnessing it the first time.

The pigs were allowed to go outside into a large enclosed area like a pasture. This pasture was surrounded with an electric fence. I was following my dad one summer day after a heavy rain. We walked down by the pig barn. When my dad came to the electric fence he was wearing gloves and he also had rubber boots on. He took a hold of the fence wire and pushed it down and swung his legs over the wire one at a time. I saw this maneuver and walked up to the wire planted my right foot firmly in 2 inches of water and grabbed hold of the wire with my right hand and stood there with one leg up in the air and one hand on the electric fence screaming at the top of my lungs. The electric fence was 110 volts. My dad by this time was 50 or 75 feet beyond the fence in the pasture. When he heard me screaming he turned around to see what had happened. When he saw that I was hung up on the electric fence he ran back as fast as he could and with his right hand fully extended hit me in the chest and pushed me off the electric fence. It took me a great many years to recover from that experience of electrocution.

Around the farm there was a great deal of equipment, machinery, scrap iron, and other things that were laying around that kids could easily get hurt on. We were however carefully instructed by our dad to be careful around the farm.We were repeatedly told that an injury could happen at any time and very suddenly. My brothers and myself were walking down in back by the pig barn on a beautiful winter day. The day was bright and sunny but the temperature was almost 0°. As we walked by at trailer that was parked in the yard in front of the pig barn Solomon, the youngest one of my brothers whowas with us decided that he wanted to lick some ice off the steel rail on the trailer. Before we could stop him he had already attempted to lick the ice. As soon as his tongue touched the ice it froze to the steel rail. Now without making any special effort we had a problem on our hands. There was no warm water anywhere around. There seem to be no convenient way to detach his tongue from the steel rail. So the two of us boys got a hold of his coat in the back and pulled him off. Of course this only serve the purpose of leaving part of his tongue attached to the steel rail. My little brother took a long time to recover from this injury. It also served the purpose of controlling his excessive talking.

Chapter 10

Winter Sports

During the winter there was and amazing amount of snow. There was also a great deal of drifting. For some reason the drifting snow piled up in quite a large area around my mothers wash line. This seemed like a perfect place for us boys to dig out a snow house in the drifted snow. We work for three or four days digging out a large snow house in the snowdrift. We were even able to dig out high enough up in the ceiling of the snow house so that my mother's wash line hung down inside the snow house. This made a great place to hang up things. At some point within the next couple of weeks someone managed to walk on top of the snowdrift I guess to see how high it was. But within a few seconds of walking on top of the snowdrift they broke through the ceiling. That pretty well destroyed our snow house.

Sledding was another much enjoyed activity of the children in the colony. Someone in the colony had built a large sled of two heavy steel runners. When we sanded the rust off the runners and waxed the bottoms of the runners with regular floor wax the sled was quite fast in the snow. We took the sled to the Hill on the western side of the property. This hill was very well suited for sledding. There was nothing blocking our sled trail at the bottom of the hill. The snow was about 2 feet deep. We had been sledding on this hill for two or three hours that day. On one run my sister Rachel was sitting up front onthe sled. Three other girls were sitting at the back just behind her. As the sled started down the hill someone decided to jump on the sled from the back. This caused the other girls to slide forward. My sister Rachel slid forward causing her leg to slide over a nail that had stock up through the sled. Nobody had ever seen this nailbefore in the sled. The nail cut a large gash in my sister's leg. She had to be tacken to a hospital to have the gash stitched up.

We also got into ice-skating on the river. The river during a cold winter froze almost solid. And most of the time the wind keped the snow cleared off of the ice. Ice skating on the river was a wonderful experience. We had acquired a number of pairs of ice skates from some friends of the colony. When we went ice skating on the river there was always a heavy breeze blowing. It was neet to skate on the river when the wind was blowing. If we held our coat out the wind would blow us down the river fairly fast. We did have to stay away from dead branches that had fallen in the river because the ice did not freeze very solidly around the wood.

The Hutterites were a farming people. Very few of the colonies got into any kind of industry. In farming there is always a large amount of equipment. The potential for injury not only to young people but also to anyone on the farm is quite high. As farming community the Hutterites had relatively few instances of injury. And whileyoung people had freedom a lot of the time to do what they wanted to, supervision was very prevalent. But as a child growing up in a Hutterites community it was a very happy childhood. I don't believe there are very many young people amongst the Hutterites that could say they had a lousy childhood. I grew up with the Hutterites only to the age of eight. But these first eight years of my life proved to be the happiest part of my childhood.

Chapter 11

The Invaders

In the early and mid-30s an outsider from Germany, by the name of Heimler, cameto visit the Hutterites. He had started a communal type lifestyle in Germany. But the number of people he had in his community was very few. The Hutterites on the other hand had between 3000 and 5000 members between Canada and United States. This Heimler tried to persuade the Hutterites to join his community to become a part of his established community. The Hutterites showed him the door and asked him kindly to leave and not to come back. This visit from this gentleman did considerable damage to the Hutterites. It became quite apparent that a lot of the young people were somewhat dissatisfied with the spiritual part of the Hutterite lifestyle and were looking for a different way of life. Heimler got his start in Germany after World War I. He ran against Hitler for control of the German youth movement. When Hitler won out and took control of the German youth movement,Heimler tried to start his own German youth movement. The problem was not very many young people want to follow him. So he decided to turn it into a community where he could have some control over some people.

Theis group in Germany was forced out of Germany by Hitler's SS troops. Heimler, who came to visit us in the mid-30s died in Germany. The rest of his community moved to England. But at the start of World War II the bombing in England caused them to move to South America, namely Paraguay. By early 1950s this group from Paraguay sent scouts to America to look for a place to build a community. They located two places one in Pennsylvania near Pittsburgh. And in another place near Rifton New York. The group from South America led by Vonkoph, the son of Heimler abandoned

31

the three communities that they had in Paraguay and moved to New York State and Pennsylvania. They abandoned a large number of their people there in Paraguay and they also abandoned a number of people in New York City at the airports and in Pittsburgh at the airport. These people that they had abandoned in Paraguay and the airports were absolutely destitute. They had no conceivable way of making a living. The ones that had been brought to the U.S. had hope of some kind through assistance programs by the city and the state. The ones that were abandoned in Paraguay had no hope of any conceivable way of making a living.

This group's contact with the Hutterites continued and in 1954 caused Forest River colony to split up. A large number of the members at Forest River left to join the community in New York State and Pennsylvania. My mother and father decided to move our family to New York State. Some of our belongings were shipped to New York State by truck. The family however had to be moved by train. Our family was taken to Grand Forks and put on a train bound for New York City. This train ride was to take three days. I was not yet 8 years old, my sister Barbara was nine, and my older sister Rachel was 10. Rachel and Barbara assisted my mom and dad to keep track of the rest of the children. Solomon was just three years old. My mom had put a harness around his chest. A leash, was attached to the back of the harness, and I had a hold of the other end of the leash. It was my job to keep track of Solomon. It was a very difficult job for us young boys to contain ourselves to one passenger car on the train. We soon discovered that there was a dining car, as well as a sleeper car. And we continually visited all of the other passengers on the entire train and made our presence known in every single car. My mother finally gave up trying to keep track of us because it occurred to her that as long as the train was moving we could not get off. This was the most exciting trip we had ever been on. I had never seen a train up close never mind having been in one. The big cities that we went through to stop and let off passengers and get new passengers on were amazing to watch through the windows. I had never been on a railroad train in my life, and these big cities had hundreds of railroad tracks. By the time we got to New York City it seemed like it took us an hour to get from the edge of the city to where the railroad tracks were and the train was going to stop.

A tall slender man met us at the train station by the name of Robertwhom we recognize as having visited Forest River colony. Our whole family was loaded into several automobiles and transported to Rifton New York and the community that had already been established. We arrived at the new community, called Pine Hill,where we were driven up to the house that we are to live in. All of our belongingshad already arrived and were sitting in boxes and suitcases in the living room.

Chapter 12

The Cult—Getting Started

The first couple of days that we were at Pine Hill were hectic at best. There were always new people showing up at our house trying to help. There were also people that showed up to instruct us about the life in the community and what was expected of us. But this language they were speaking, English I didn't know.Most of the kids in the family did not know English. My sister Rachel and Barbara had learned how to speak some of it. I realize from the very beginning that this new community was not only different but there was something about it that was not quite right. I was only seven years old but I could already sense spiritual concepts and spiritual attitudes. I could sense the spirit in people when talking with them or watching them.From the verybeginning at Pine Hill I learned very quickly that watching other people very carefully was to benefit me greatly.It did not take very long for me to be able to pick out the people in the community that were going to be my friends as well as those who were going to be my enemies. This concept of having friends as well as enemies in a community had never before occurred to me. It was just not a part of our life at the Hutterites. But in Pine Hill it seemed like there were people therewho were late teens or early 20s and older who seem to enjoy going out of their way to bully me or just to make things difficult for my brothers and me. And I think that the problem was that we were so much different than other people around us, that they saw the difference but didn't know how to react to it. I was very often seen even as a young boy as being different by people around. With the Hutterites this caused me problems until most people just figured that I was just a little weird. As I was to learn at a later date the difference they saw in me was seen as me as having a bad attitude.

Bad attitudes in this new community were not tolerated and every effort was made from the very beginning to subdue what they saw as a bad attitude. For me the struggles from the very beginning became a struggle for my survival. From the very beginning at Pine Hill a lot of people stared at us as if we were from Mars. It was very obvious that some people in this community saw something extremely odd in us. My two brothers just younger than me also ran into this problem. With my two younger brothers they were guilty by association with me.

We could always get away for a while and go exploring. We soon learned that our going to explore was a wonderful way to get away from people we consideredour enemies. School at Pine Hill was already in session. And we were expected within a couple of days to be in school. After sorting out what grade we belonged in primarily by our age, we were instructed on where to go to school. There were in Pine Hill some compassionate adults that kept an eye on us. They perceived from the very beginning that english was not our best-spoken language. But within a few months time we began to understand and even be able to speak some english. But the other kids continually made fun of us and taunt of us. Some of the adults saw our difficulties merely are having a bad attitude. Every time a problem showed up with us it seemed to come back to the point of just having a bad attitude. I had never heard of a bad attitude before never mind that I was suspected of having one. In my opinion as an seven-year-old I didn't even have any kind of an attitude. Never mind a bad one. My mom and dad were so involved in establishing themselves in this community that they didn't have time to properly instruct us in the tremendous change that we were experiencing. Ben and John who were just younger than me had a little bit of a learning problem. Within the first two or three months this problem showed up. At first they were also labeled as having a bad attitude and being rebellious. It soon became apparent that they would need extra help to get started. By the time this problem was finally recognized considerable damage had already occurred. The first winter in this weird community was really quite difficult.

Some of the teachers in the school system in Pine Hill saw the problems that we were having. But they were also the ones who associated our problems with having a bad attitude and being rebellious. Eventually we were set aside and put in a room by ourselves because they did not want us to be a bad influence on the other children. This isolation lasted for about three months. But it was long enough to let us know that we were not quite welcome. That first winter seemed like it lasted for 10 years. It seemed like that first winter would never end. When spring and summer finally came school finally let out. We found out very quickly that the freedoms we had known with the Hutterites were no longer there. Every single day for the children from eight o'clock in the morning to six or seven a clock at night was planned in advance. And the only thing for us to do was to go along with the preplanned days and grit our teeth and bear it. It took us children over a year to become acclimated to Pine Hill. It was around the beginning of the second year in school that Jack Stein took over as the head of the school. In the very beginning this man was fairly easy-going. It seemed as though he was the right man to oversee a bunch of children in school. Jack Stein was a large man of about 275 to 300 pounds. Considering his weight he was extremely agile and could move fairly quickly when he had to.

In Pine Hill breakfast was always eaten with the families in their home. Lunch and dinner were eaten in a collective dining room. With the Hutterites the collective dining room the men eat on one side of the room and the women and young girls eat on the other side. With this weird community everybody was all mixed up. My two younger brothers and myself were almost always very closely watched. We were very closely watched it seemed like by almost everyone in the community. I was especially closely watched. I do not think that we could have been more closely watched if we had had some serious disfiguring deformity. It was almost as though people in this community had never seen anything quite like us before.

It was during the summer of this first year at Pine Hill when the Lord first spoke to me. I knew from Bible study at the Hutterites that God frequently talk to people. But he had never talked to me before. The conversation that the Lord had with me started very simply. The Lord said"David". I looked around to see who had called my name. I was alone and there was no one else around. After a few minutes I heard my name called again. Again I looked around to try to find out who was calling my name. The third time the Lord called my name I answered and asked who is it that is calling my name. The Lord answered me and said "I am the Lord God of your people Israel. I have called you to be a prophet. You will go where I send you and you will speak what I cause you to speak". I simply replied to the Lord and said, "I have never done anything like this before ". Again the Lord told me "you will go to whom I send you and you will speak what I cause you to speak". This was definitely a different conversation than speaking with real people. But I kept this conversation to myself because at the time people thought I was weird enough. If they knew that God was talking to me who knows what might happen. I was already considered as someone with a bad attitude and rebellion. How much worse would my situation get if I told them that God had talked to me. These people were supposed to be Christians they were supposed to believe in the Bible. They were supposed to believe that God calls people to be prophets and that God used messengers too. But in my spirit I knew full well that if I told anyone of the conversation that I had just had with the Lord my life would never be the same. And the persecution I knew was going to start soon enough and I did not want to assist anyone in persecuting me

Chapter 13

The Lord Calls Me To Service

My life went on as normally as it could.From that point on I did not hear from the Lord again for about four or five months. The man who was considered the leader of Pine Hill was Vonkoph the son of Heimler, who had visited the Hutterites. He had his office upstairs in the main building. His second-in-command Frank Mosley had his office just down the hall from the Heimler's. The second time the Lord spoke to me was in the middle of the afternoon towards the end of the summer of the first year. The Lord said I was supposed to go to Frank Mosley and he called him by name.The Lord would tell me what to say when I got into his office. I didn't even hesitate I went to the men's office. The door was closed so I knocked and walked in. When the man behind the desk looked up and said to me what is it that you want. I said "the Lord God of my people has sent me to bring you a message". So the looked at me with a swagger of his head "all right what's the message". All of the worship services in this cult were done in secret behind closed doors. Only members were allowed to attend. I was not a member. But as I started talking to this man the Lord gave me the message I was supposed to deliver to him. I said to him "the Lord told me that this is the message, that you preached from the Bible last night. The scripture that you read, you read incorrectly. The message that you preached based on this scripture was also incorrect". And I proceeded to explain to this man where his error in his preaching had been and what the truth that he should have preached was. And I turned around and left his office. I never heard another word about that first visit. But this experience opened my eyes to what was really going on with the management of this community.

I started to intensely watch the leaders of this community and the people who were running the operation. I discovered very quickly that the headman was not living a very Christian life.I was used by the Lord in this manner to prophesy to this particular man, Frank Mosley on three other occasions. I sincerely believe that it was these occasions that the Lord used me as a messenger for him to the leadership that initially started the intense interrogations that I endured. These interrogation sessions,as I called them, were actually attempted brainwashing sessions.

The Group of Brothers as these people call themselves, did not make their living by farming. They did have a large vegetable garden. But this was totally for their own use. They had a factory in which they produce child size furniture and educational equipment and toys. This equipment and toys was sold to Catholic schools as well as well-established private schools. When we arrived at Pine Hill this factory was just getting started. And this is where my father worked. After school and during times when we didn't have anything else to do even the younger children were expected to be in this factory to help out. I don't believe that I actually started working in the factory until I was at least 10 years old. Those boys that did not work in a factory were expected to help out in the garden. That's whereBen and John and myself spent a lot of our time. We also spent a lot of time around Pine Hill cleaning up, raking leaves and keeping the outside groomed and cared for. Ben and John and myself, whenever we had time and could get away spent a lot of time walking around the place explored. Our times of exploration grew in time as well as in distance. We started exploring the woods. We could keep track of where we were and how to get back by trail markers we left. It didn't take very long for us to know the full layout of the surrounding countryside. And our exploration went a mile or two beyond the actual community.

During one of these ventures of exploring in the woods over a mile away from the community we discovered an old log cabin in the woods. This is where we spent quite a bit of time hanging out. This became our spot away from people and the weird community. We even started to leave supplies in his cabin such as paperplates and spoons. We even found a small coffee pot that was up there. I guess all three of us in the back of her mind had the same thought.

Someday we just might need to get away from the place and might need some supplies. I sincerely believe that these times spent away from the community was set up by God to keep us secure and to keep us somewhat isolated. Whoever had built this cabin in the woods had done a very good job. The roof did not leak and the cabin had a wooden floor. The cabin was also outfitted with a wood stove.

It was during the second winter after the start of the second's school year, that the worst of my problems in this community started. I was singled out to be talked to by the elders of the community. These meetings they started having with me started out fairly simply and almost innocently. Like somebody was supposed to be looking after us when they lost track of us wanted to know where we went. The questioning was fairly straightforward. About what I like to do, what I like to talk about the most, what I liked or didn't like about the community.Even as detailed as what kinds food I like to eat. If I enjoyed working in the shop.Even if I like the other people around me or the other kids. It seemed to me from the very beginning that they were really looking for information about me that they did not want to ask me about directly. This first session only last about an hour to an hour and a half. But within a few days I was called back for another one of the sessions. The second session started out with more questions about myself. Questions about my family and my other brothers and sisters. But very soon took a turn more along the lines of indoctrination. During these interrogation sessions to questioning turned and became accusations. I was being accused of having wrong relationships with boys as well as girls. I was intently questioned as to whether I had ever been alone for any length of time with any of the girls in the community. I was also told about this time that because my attitude was so bad that people in the community were having a great deal of trouble dealing with me. This line of questioning and accusations continued for quite a while. These sessions started to occur quite frequently. 2 to 3 days a week and as often as five days a week. From as little as an hour and a half or two hours to as much as 8 to 10 hours a day constant questioning without a break. Sometimes it was only two maybe three men doing the drilling, to as many as five and even six men, two and sometimes three of them speaking at the same time. The questioning continued along the same lines but changed very slightly. Very soon the questions took on the form of why I had become involved in a wrong or evil relationship. I was informed that I had been seen with a girl alone when we thought we were out of sight from anyone. This went on for quite a few sessions. Another turn in the line of questioning and accusations started to become apparent. The turn in questioning and accusations took on a very sinister characteristic. The attempt now was to let me know how evil I really was. I was told in no uncertain terms that I was to evil for God to save me. The attempt of these interrogation sessions was to totally break down my confidence in what I had been taught all my life concerning my salvation through faith in the shed blood of Christ. It was also an attempt to let me know that God would want nothing to do with me because I was so evil. It was at about this time in these interrogation sessions that the attempt was made to indoctrinate me with new and different ideas concerning my understanding of Scripture.The stress in me started to build and started to show quite plainly at home. My mother thought at first that I was becoming ill. The first reaction she had was to send me to the doctor. The doctor assured her that there was nothing wrong with me. But the session started to show up in me in a very dramatic way. I started very quickly, towards the end of the second winter developing a nervous breakdown. I found it very difficult to endure these constant sessions of interrogation. By this time I knew what they were after. They were trying to change my way of thinking, believing, or comprehending spiritual matters. I had to find a way to counteract. I never found a way to stop it or counteract this on my own. The Lord however gave me a unique ability of psychoanalyzing the men while they were attempting to indoctrinateme. While these men were questioning me I discovered that by carefully watching them and listening to them I could connect with them spiritually. I could also access their consciousness and very quickly learned how they thought, how they feltand things that they believe in. This new talent that the Lord gave me was the ability to be able to operate in the spiritual realm. My spiritual ability to see and hear in the spirit was dramatically increased. As these men were questioning me I could see how their spirit operated. This ability from this point forward in my life would be extremely useful.These men were all hipocrites. They talked very nicley about their Christian faithand believe when people were listening, but when they thought no one was watching they lived totally different. These sessions however never stopped. They lasted for the rest of the time that I was at this community. I got to the point with a nervous breakdown thatI trembled so badly that I had a hard time putting food in my mouth. I found it almost impossible to hold a glass of milk or water in one hand. I never drank coffee with sugar in it because I couldn't get the sugar to my coffees. My writing was never very good to start with but now it was totally illegible. Even if the people in the school got me to print it was 90% illegible. Almost all of my other behavior while around people took a similar track. This continued to deteriorate until I was in a state of almost total dysfunction. But I also discovered that while away from people and exploring with my brothers I was quite okay. My brothers also experienced similar treatment but not nearly as harsh

Chapter 14

Learning How To Survive

Ben and John and myself decided that maybe it was time for us to spend more time away from the community by ourselves. The cabin that we had found in the woods was over a mile away from the community. Nobody else in the community knew about this cabin. We were very sure that nobody had ever followed us when we had gone out to the cabin. We spent some time for the next few weeks fixing up the cabin. We got plastic to put over the Windows; we fixed up a makeshift door. The cabin also had a small wood stove inside. We made sure that the stovepipe went through the roof without hitting any wood. We tried the stovepipe by building a fire in the stove. The smoke ventted out very well. The stove was just what we needed to keep the place warm. We also spent time stacking firewood close to the cabin so that it was available for our use. We also spent some time gathering supplies. Every time we came to the cabin from this point on we brought in things that we thought we would need. We managed to acquire plates, cups, knives, and forks, as well as some warmer clothing and other things we thought that we would need. Now what we needed to find a way to do was to get together some food supplies. This is going to be a little bit harder. By trial and error we came up with a plan that seemed to work. We would start bringing up items that were caned food or food in jars that had been preserved. Perishable foodstuffs we could always bring up, as we needed them. We worked out a plan so that we had enough supplies at this cabin just in case we want to make a run for it. We even went so far as to plan how to run away.

That first summer that we spent at this community was one of the most difficult I have ever spent in my life. Because of the constant interrogations that were going on with me, also because of the abuse that my two younger brother suffered almost nonstop. The abuse that the three of us were suffering almost nonstop seem to be isolated to just the three of us. As we watched other children in the community none of them ever suffered the kind of abuse that the three of us did. We spent as much time as we could away from everybody. The way we reasoned it out was that if we were not around anyone else we couldn't very well cause any trouble. This however did not solve the problem. We also made a promise to each other that the three of us or at least two of us would be together all the time. The only time that we would become separated was if one of us was sick and the other two had to continue in school or other activities. This strategy worked quite well. We discovered very quickly that less persecution came against us if there were three of us. Now there were always two witnesses. This stopped a lot of the personal attacks that were coming against us from one or two people at a time that we just happen to run into. We also developed a skill of hiding in plain sight. We learned how to stay out of people's focal point while in the midst of a group of other kids. What we didn't realize at the time was that we were acquiring survival skills that would help us a great deal later on in life. How to be in a crowd and not to be visibly seen. This was starting to save us a great deal of unnecessary persecution and personal attacks.

The school year of 1956 to 1957 started towards the middle of the end of September. This was going to be a very difficult trying time because now for most of the day we were separated. While the personal attacks came against us from other children, they were nowhere near as bad as the attacks we suffered from adults. We could almost cope with these. The problem we all three had in school was that it was difficult for us at times to pay attention. Our minds were always working to try to figure a way to get through the next round of interrogation or the next persecution that was to come against us by adults on the place. My two younger brothers suffered far worse then I did. Because of the distraction trying to find a way through the day that lay ahead they suffer tremendously in schoolwork. The problem we had was that we had not acquired much English school instruction in North Dakota. But this instruction had not prepared us for the total English school that we were now getting. And we were still struggling to learn how to speak English. Between ourselves we still spoke the Austrian that we had spoken all our life. All the while this was going on at school my mom and dad were getting bad reports from the teachers about us. We tried to explain the situation to them and while my father was very receptive and tried to give us some advice on how to cope my mother kind of turned her back and didn't pay too much attention to us. So it looked like we were kind of on our own except for some advice that our dad had given us. But dad's advice was always very good and always worked.

Ben and John had a much more severe problem in school. The pain and suffering they went through had considerably diminished their ability to study.During this year of school they were assigned to a woman who was tutoring them. With this woman's assistance they seem to be making fairly good progress. The other nice thing about this woman spending so much time with them to try to teach them and help them out was that they were not with all the other children. This isolation from the other children help them out to the degree that they were not taunted,jeeredat or bullied. With this method this study they seem to progress nicely.

The school was set off to one side of the central community buildings. To the front of the school towards the dining room there was a large front lawn. During the winter when the first heavy snow fell a lot of children got out on the front lawn and shoveled snow around the edges of the lown. This was done to form a damn around the lawn. The lawn was then flooded with water and allow freezing. When the ice got thick enough and hard enough it made a good skating rink. The three of us had already learned how to skate in North Dakota. At this new community there were never enough ice skates to go around. So some of us had to borrow skates from other children. This should never have been a problem because the children them selves did not own the skates. It was however a problem for us three because we were always told that there were not any skates available right now. But the right now never changed. So we found out that if we were going to do any skating it had to be after everybody else was in bed asleep. This policy works very well because there was always light on the front lawn skating rink. And there was never anyone around to bother us. This wasquite a successful policy during his first winter. If anyone saw us we would just tell themthat we were trying to enjoy a few minutes of stating. That seemed to satisfy them.

Thanksgiving of that year and Christmas and Easter came and went without any additional difficulties. The three of us seem to be learning how to live without having a bad attitude. Although from time to time we were reminded that we weren't normal. We were still reminded almost continually of being in rebellion.

Chapter 15

Attacks Become Personal And
With Purpose

In the summer of 1956 the community acquired an old school bus. This bus was used to go on what became known as all day trips. All of the children from fifth grade up through eighth grade could go on these trips. Lunch and dinner would be put in the bus enough for the children.We were all required to take what personal belongings we needed to take. We would leave the community at seven o'clock in the morning. We took trips up into the Catskills. We could always find a nice creek up there that had some very good swimming holes and picnic areas. To the three of us this was an incredibly wonderful experience. We're learning how to survive mostly on our own separated as much as we could be from the other people around us. Up in the Catskills the three of us could get lost for most of the day and nobody would miss us. It's incredible but for the three of us survival became an every day effort and acquired always new daily strategy. But by this time we were becoming quite good at this. Especially in summer when we were away from the rest of the group of children exploring around the shop, or almost anywhere else.If anadult saw us, we became quite good at explaining our way out of a tight predicament.The third trip that summer into the Catskills was supposed to be an overnight camping trip. We were all instructed that we would need bedrolls and warmer clothes and to be prepared to stay overnight. This is going to be an awesome trip and we three boys started enjoying it before it ever started. All of our supplies were loaded into the bus on the night before. The next morning when all the kids were getting on the bus one of the men in charge of the community came up to me just as I was getting ready to get on the bus and told me that I would not be able to go.Because of my bad attitude I had to stay home. I was escorted up to the leader's office. For 10 hours on that day six grown man interrogated me. This was especiallya bad session for me first of all because I missed the all-day trip with an overnightcamping. But also because this session by six men for 10 hours made me understand in no uncertain terms that I was evil, that I had demons in me, and that I was not somebody that God would even consider allowing to be saved. I was given to understand that I was the most undesirable human being on the face of the earth and that this community had the undesirable task of caring for me until the devil came to get me. Because at this point it was made absolutely crystal clear to me that God would never want the likes of me in heaven. I was also informed at this interrogation session that I was the devil's agent. After this session I stole some food from the kitchen and went to the cabin in the woods and stayed there for two days. After two days when I came home people were considerably worried. My mother and father both wanted to know where I'd gone. I explain to them as carefully as I could that I had gone on my own overnight camping trip. That I felt I'd been cheated out of it for no good reason.That what was happening to me was coming very close to destroying me. My complaining at this point got back to the management of the community and I was completely taken out of the children's community. My mother had betrayed me to the leadership.

Chapter 16

Internal Exile And Slave Labor

I was told that because I was causing so much trouble in the school that I would have to spend all of my time during the day from now on working in their factory. I was also told at this meeting that because I was the devil's agent I could not be around the other children. This became my first experience with slave labor. I was in the factory working not because of a normal work schedule but to get me out of the way. This forced labor seem to be an answer for the management of this community to temporarily dispose of me. It was during this part of my life when the thought of ending my life first came to mind. It seemed to me that I was not serving a very useful purpose in my existence. It also seems to me that if I was so much trouble to everyone around me that the best thing for me to do was to end my existence. At the same time that these thoughts were going through my mind I realized that God had already used me on a number of occasions as a messenger for him. If God thought that I was good enough for him to use as a messenger then what was the problem with the people around me. This conflict started to work on me and did not leave me alone. I had to seek the Lord for a solution. The solution however evaded me for a considerabley long time.

This internal exile lasted most of the summer. School was in session for a full month before I was allowed to return to school. But in school I was also isolated for a short period of time. But it became inconvenient for the school to keep me isolated so I was allowed to go back to the regular classroom with the other kids. During the next school year while I was with the rest of the children was still extremely trying. While I was allowed to be with the rest of the children in school I was still in internal exile. I was also very much excluded by other children. Almost all of the other kids kept their distance from the.

Nobody was allowed to associate with me or talk to me. This internal exile lasted most of the winter. Even by the end of the school year things did not improve very much. The following summer I discovered that my association with the rest of the children in the community would be extremely limited. It was required that most of my time be spent working in the factory. For the most part most of the men in the factory had already been instructed not to associate with me. It also seems to me that most of the men in this factory had been instructed to make things as difficult for me as they possibly could. Out of 30 or 35 men that made up the workforce in his factory there were only two or three that actually looked at me with some degree of human kindness. Whenever I try to associate with a man in his factory they would walk away. Even at coffee break in the morning and in the afternoon if I sat down next to one of the men they always got up and walked away. My father who worked in the factory and two other men were the only ones who ever associated wi

Chapter 17

Brutality Beyond Belief

This summer was to prove to be the most difficult I had lived so far. I spent a good part of the summer working in the factory. The times when I got out of the factory for a few days at a time I spent with my two younger brothers. I believe that it was July of that year when things took a turn for the worse. The two brothers and myself started an egg collection. The eggs came from birds that laid eggs in their nests. The point was to get as many different kinds of eggs as we could find. The way we accomplish this was to watch birds build their nests. By observation we knew when they were ready to lay eggs. As soon as the birds had laid an egg we would get an egg out of the nest. We would punch a hole in each end of the egg. This allowed us to blow the egg yolk and the whites out of the egg. We were left with a completely intact shell. This was a good way to collect different kinds of eggs. We realize that the egg should be fertil but we did not see a problem with collecting eggs the way we were. The baby birds had not started to develop yet. We needed an egg from a Robin. We knew whare a robin's nest was in the big pine tree in front of the school. On a sunny afternoon we climbed the tree and got out an egg. This egg had just been laid. No baby bird had started to develop yet. We punched a hole in each end of the egg as we had done in all the others that we collected. We blew out the insides of the egg and had a complete eggshell.Jack Stein, who was in charge of the school, saw us doing this. He came over to where we were and accused us of killing baby birds. This of course was not true, as the baby birds had not yet started to develop. Jack Stein was 6 foot tall and weighed well over 275 pounds. He was very well muscled out. Jack Steintook Ben and John and myself down in back of the school. There was a grove of pine trees in back of the school with several picnic tables underneath them. There were some dead pine loges along the edges. He sent us down on the pine logs. He proceeded to lecture us on how wrong it was to kill baby bird's fresh out of the nest. This is again something that we had never done or evercontemplated doing. While he spoke to us he picked up a dead pine branch. This dry pine stick was about an inch and a half in diameter, Over 2 feet long. He very carefully smoothed it out with a penknife and cut off all of the small branches that stuck out from it.Hetook Ben by the arm and dragged him over to the table. He bent my brother over the picnic table and proceeded to beat him viciously with the pine stick. Jack Stein had considerable strength in his arms. It appearedto John and myself that he was using all of his force on each blow that he delivered to Ben'sback,buttocks, and legs down to the knees. At first my brother screamed in agony as these merciless blows continued to rain down on him with no end in sight.After another two or three blows Ben stopped screaming. As his limp body hung on the picnic table Jack Stein continued to rain down blows with no sign of mercy. After what seemed like 100 blows had been delivered my brother John and I got upoff the log into a standing position. We each had penknives in our pockets that had 4-inch blades. My dad had taught us how to sharpen these knife. John and I with the blades open and in our right-hand made advances on Jack Stein who was still beating my brother. We raised our arms with our knives in our hands and came towards him. When we were two steps away fromJack Stein, he suddenly stopped beating my brother. He dropped his stick on the ground turned around and looked at us and promptly walked out of the pinewoods. At this point my brother was no longer conscious. His shirt and pants were bloody. When we called his name and try to revive him he just lay limply on the picnic table.John and myself pick Ben up and dragged him home. We had one of his arms over our shoulder and hung onto his belt in his pants. All the way home his feet drag the ground he never regained consciousness. People who saw us crossing the community draggingBen this way never offered any assistance or ask us if there was something wrong. When we gotto the house my mother and my sisters Rachel and Barbara were there. We took my brother into his bedroom and laid him facedown on the bed. My mother very carefully stripped his clothes off him. The shert had to be cut off. The welts and lacerations on my brothers back went from just below his shoulder blades all the way down to his knees. The swelling of these welts had already started. The discoloration of the skin followed very quickly and became a very deep blue almost black. The welts left on his back were bleeding quite severely. My brother was nine years old.

For the next two weeksBen lay in bed on his face. It took three days before he regained consciousness. No doctor ever came to treat my brother. He very nearly died. For two weeks we had to change the sheets under his crippled body. He couldn't even get up to go to the bathroom. Every time my mother went to treat and clean wounds he screamed in agony. The only thing Ben could eat for the first week was broth. He urinated a considerable amount of blood. How he survived I have no idea. His survival was a miracle by the healing hand of God. This situation like so many times before, God again showd us incredible favor. The grace and mercy of our God touched my brother during his healing process. This healing process took considerable time in his body's ability to mend the wounds. The healing for myself and my brother John would take many many long years and would never be totally accomplished apart from God's personal intervention in my life at least.

Not a single person in the community ever asked me where John about this incident. As far as I'm aware the management of this community never questioned Jack Stein or took any action to punish him for almost beating my brother to death. Jack Stein continued to be around the community and continued to be the head of the school.

From that moment on I learned how to hate. I hated specifically, personally, distinctly, with passion and purpose. My hate was directed at three specific individuals. From that moment on my desire and purpose of my life was to suspend the life of these three people. From this moment forward I taught myself at every opportunity how to put a man down and how to kill him. I became quite adept at fighting with my feet. I was 10 years old when this happened.I spent a great deal of time waiting for an opportunity to strike. I got very comfortable looking over my shoulder continually. If I could help it I never allowed myself to get into a situation that I could not get out of fast. Up until this point in my life I didn't even know what hate was. My little brother took considerable months to recover from this violent, insane, without a reason, beating to within one stroke of his life. He was never the same after that. This beating completely changed him. By the time he was fully recovered he had no memory whatsoever of his beating. The other strange thing about the beating that my brother got was that nobody else in the community seems to know anything about it. Somehow the leadership of the community had completely silenced everybody that knew anything about this.

Chapter 18

More Children In Lockup

That next school year was again difficult. I was once again in isolation and internal exile. It was during this next school year that the management of the community decided to have what they call a clearing session. All the schoolchildren were supposed to tell each other what bad feelings they had against each other. This for me was a very great waste of time. I had bad feelings against a lot of those children because of the way we were mistreated continually. The way I look at it if that wasn't obvious enough then what good would it do for me to verbalize it.There were six other children in the school that felt the same way I did. It wasn't very long, within a week or 10 days after this clearing session started that the seven of us were isolated. All seven of us were exiled and not allowed to communicate or associate with anyone else in the community. For six months we were locked up in a small room at the school. This room was just big enough for seven desks. There was no window, only one door that was kept locked while we were in the room. There was also one electric light permitted in this room. I was the oldest boy in there at ten; the youngest was six years old.

This excommunication and lock up lasted for six months. We were allowed to go home at night. And we had to be back to be locked up during the day at seven o'clock in the morning. Lunch was served to us in lockup. Once in the morning and once in the afternoon someone came in and unlocked the door to see if any of us needed to go to the bathroom. No water or anything else was offered to us during the day. The room that we are locked into was almost totally dark. There was no internal light and the external light had been blocked off. We were not allowed to talk to each other or even whisper to each other. We were not allowed to knock on the door to get anyone's attention from outside. Another words haveing a bathroom break had to happen it had to happen where we were sitting.From time to time a large German man named Hermancame in to check on us. If one of us was caught whispering we got slapped in the back of the head. Or our knuckles were severely clipped with the edge of a ruler. We soon recognized by the squeak of the floorboards when this guy was coming. But on oneoccasion Herman showed up with no warning. A little boy sitting to my right was just six years old.He was whispering to me trying to tell me that he had to go to bathroom. I tried to get him to be still but he continued to whisper. When a Herman came in the room he saw this little boy whispering.Herman reached over with his right hand and by the hair of this little boy's head yanked him up into the air. He held this little boy by his hair suspended in midair. With his left hand he proceeded to slap this little boy across the face back and forth a dozen times. I finally got up out of my chair and came over to him. When he saw me coming and standing in front of him with my fists raised, Herman viciously through Jimmy back down in his chair. He then turned around and stormed out of the room. Locking the door behind him. This little boy had to make a bathroom break right where he was sitting. I can not for the life of me imagine what a six-year-old boy could possibly have done that would merit locking this little boy up for six months. How could this little child's behavior be so far out of control that he had to be treated in this manner. Jimmy was one of the nicest and best behaved little children that I had encountered at this community. If anyone in the world could possibly have had a complaint against Jimmy it would have had to have been made up and totally fabricated.

The brutality of the treatment that I witnessed by a dozen different individuals in this community defies logic, reason, purpose, and common sense. Pine Hill was supposed to be Christian. When complaints were made to management concerning the brutality of these people it was hushed up. The complaints were never acted on. Nothing was ever done. I find it very difficult to believe that this kind of brutality occurred anywhere else in secular society. But to find it occurring in a Christian community is mind-boggling.So many times I witnessed when a child asked a simple question he was backhanded by a full-grown man's hand swung with force and knocked to the ground. Very often this child walked away bleeding from the mouth. Where in society had these brutes grown up? It is not possible to comprehend that these people had any prior experience with children or life in the community of any kind never mind a Christian community.

This lockup that we were confined to lasted for six months. After six months the will of the management of the community seem to have been broken. Because we were told that our confinement would end. But we were told not to get the idea that we got away with anything. It just seems like a waste of time to keep some worthless kids like you locked up any longer. Becouse they said this is costing us a lot of extra work and extra money. So without the community having gained anything by the six-month lockup they let us out and let us return to what was left of the school year, which was not very much. Every single one of the children that was a part of this lockup was dramatically changed for the rest of their life. This six month confinement made a dramatic difference in all of these children. This difference was by no means an improvement on their character or personality. The damage that was caused in this six month confinement would either need extensive help at a later time in their life or just be a part of their character forever.

Chapter 19

God Provides A Defense

I believe it was in the summer of 1960 when the fire happened. The main building at Pine Hill, which housed the kitchen, dining room, Vonkoph's office, and Frank Mosley's office, caught fire. This fire almost completely destroyed the building. It was quite apparent that an entirely new building would have to be constructed. It seemed almost ironic to me that after a display of such brutality against some of the most innocent people in Pine Hill and against former Hutterites who are already God's people that this main building was leveled by fire. Seems almost like God was trying to tell these people something. The problem was nobody was listening. Down in back of the main building was a large level field that we had turned into a baseball field. A bunch of us kids had been down on this field shortly after the main building was completed, playing ball. When we came up from the ball field, we walked up the bank along one end of the main building. One of the girls was running up this hill when her right foot dragged over the end of a large frayed piece of cable that was sticking out of the ground about 10 inches. Before she could stop she had dragged her foot over the end of this piece of cable. The cable literally shredded her foot on top. The individual wires in the cable cut so deep in her foot that the bones were exposed. We got her up to the top of the hill and tried to pick her up the carrier to the doctor's office. The young lady refused to allow us to carry her. This girl was probably 8 or 9 years old. Some of the men who were coming out of the main building saw us,came over and picked the young lady up and carried her over to the doctor's office.She was very severely injured. When this injury occurred I experienced excruciating pain in my right foot as if my foot had been the one that was cut. I did not understand how

58

I could feel somebody else's physical pain. But this was to play an important part later on in my life. Again I got in trouble for this incident as if I had caused it. It seemed like any reason no matter what it was how big or small as long as it could be used to get me into trouble was justifiable.

By the next summer I was 11 years old. I was also better equipped to take care of myself. I had learned to fight and protect myself from physical assault. When physical assault would occur I very quickly struck back with all the force I could muster. As much as possible I struck back with my feet. The continued interrogation never stopped. Missing all day trips with the rest of the children also never stopped. I missed more trips then I went on. If these interrogation sessions only lasted for a couple of hours I was required for the rest of the day to work in the shop. When I was in the shop I was expected to do a full-grown man's work. No slacking off or becoming tired before the end of the day. I was also told that I could not associate or talk to any of the men at the factory. Coffee breaks were never allowed to be with other men. My father's uncle worked in this factory and took some compassion on me. Quite a bit of the time when I was in the factory I spent time with them. And I'm absolutely sure that he saw the mistreatment that I was suffering. Because quite often he tried to talk to me and to console me and to tell me that this was not going to go on very much longer. And at the time I didn't understand what he is talking about. This continual battle in a secure Christian community was just for survival. This continual battle was not spiritual warfare as is the case quite often with a lot of individuals. This battle was solely for the purpose of surviving to the next day. I had also acquired a new talent to prove to be very helpful. Because of these continued interrogation sessions I had learned how to analyze people around the. This talent of analyzing people opened my spiritual eyes on enough so that I could see and hear in the spirit realm. This allowed me to be aware of people's intention that came into my presence. I discovered very quickly that this talent gave me a considerable advantage.

During this summer I found ways to get away by myself. My absence in the shop was seen and reported. I knew that this would mean some form of retribution. But the choice between suffering on a continual basis at the hand of other people or spending a day by myself I chose to spend the day by myself. The price is going to have to be paid anyway one way or the other. This way at least was beneficial for some people. The choice to run away with my two brothers came up on a number of occasions. We talked about it but the two younger brothers were by this time too insecure. Besides my second youngest brother who had received the incredible beating hadnot yet fully recovered.There was another activity that we became involved in. The community had acquired a number of bicycles. At least a couple of days a week we were able to get the bicycles and the three of us would pedal 5 miles to town. Money was not impossible to come by. If we kept our eyes open we always get a hold of two or three dollars. In 1955 and 1956 two or three dollars would buy a lot of candy. The other activities we became involved in were to go down by the river and go fishing. We didn't have any fishing equipment but we discovered that if we went down by the river and walked we could usually find what we needed. And we always came home with fish.

We would always meet other fishermen at the river who were fishing for special fish. They use dough balls for bait. These dough balls were made out of corn meal. By talking to them we discovered that they were fishing for carp. Just up the river was a hydroelectric dam. Every once in a while the dam overflowed. When it toverflowed a lot of carp whent overthetop. These carp became caught in rock pools below the dam. My brothers and I swam across the river and caught carp. My little brother would go into the rock pools and catch these carp by hand. Some of these carp weigh between 10 and 15 pounds. We swam back across the river with the carp in towel. The fishermen who had been sitting at their spot fishing for carp all day long saw us coming. When we came out of the water carrying three huge carp they got mad. They threw their fishing poles into river and stormed off.

This gave to us a good supply of fishing poles. But where in the world were wegoing to hide three nice fishing poles with reels and other tackle. Down close to the river Pine Hill owned a small building that was used as a pump house for their water supplies. The pump house was never locked up. And it was very seldom supervised. We found that if we stored our fishing poles in this pump house that nobody ever bothered them. A new great way to stay out of sight and out of harms way. This method of staying away work very well. If anyone came looking for us there were many places to hide.

These fishing trips wetook along the river were wonderful distraction from the life in the community. By this time in the community we had been terribly isolated. And while almost everyone that we encountered was polite to us, at the same time they shunned us. We were not treated the same as other children our age in the community. The three of us especially were treated as a burden that had to be tolerated for now because there was no other solution for us available. There were so many nice fishing spots along that stretch of the river.There was a neat old covered bridge right near there that was well enough preserved to walk across. We started spending quite a bit of time in summer along this river. It also seemed to us that when we spend time away from the community we were never missed. I suppose everybody figured that we were somewhere being supervised by somebody but they didn't rightly know who. This policy worked very nicely for us. It gave us freedom to wander and explore and at the same time kept us out of striking range whenever adults had on one else to pick on. I however discovered very quickly that this was not an answer to my problem. since the first time the Lord had used me as a messenger my spiritual insight seem to have increased considerably. This gave me the ability to sense people's true purpose in their dealings with me. The true purpose of the Elders treatment of me was to cause my demise in one form or another. My main purpose in life at this particular point was to survive.

The elders of the community were constantly watching us. While the time spent away from the community center relieved us of the psychological pressure of being constantly under surveillance, it was not an answer to our problem. Whenever the elders of the community wanted me for a special session of interrogation they had to send out someone to search for me. This made things even more difficult during the next session that I had to endure. My two younger brothers were spared these interrogations. My first real encounter with Jesus Christ was when I was eight years old and called for the first time as a prophet of the Lord. It was from that point on when I started watching carefully the activities of the

Elders in the community that I discovered how hypocritical they were in everything that they did. I also had a Bible that was given to me when I was five years old and still lived with the Hutterites. I knew by reading the word of God that there was something very wrong with the Christian beliefs that this community held. The other thing that started becoming more clear was that these people were trying to cause my demise. Preferably at my own hand.

I started watching the leader of this community very closely. I would make regular trips during the day whenever I could get away and not be seen by too many people, up into the hallway where his office was. On a number of these strips as I was in the hallway watching and listening I saw a young woman 18 to 21 years old coming out of the leader's office pulling her skirt back down and buttoning her blouse. This encounter happened not only with one young woman but also with twoothers that I knew from the community. These encounters really started to bother me. I didn't know what to do with this information so I kept it to myself and continued to watch. The behavior of these three young women that I countered leaving the leader's office in this manner changed drastically. They were no longer the same friendly young women that I had encountered in the community before. They became more and more guarded and withdrawn. They also appear to be in a state of total confusion. I learned a lot later in life, after I had left Pine Hill that all three of these young women disappeared completely. No one ever heard from them or saw them again.

There were other such behaviors that I started to observe with the leaders of this community. The elders seem to have special treatment in many areas. If everything in the community was to be shared equally amongst its members how come the elders dressed so much better than everyone else. How come the food they ate was so much better than the food everyone else ate? Everyone in the community seems to be equal with the exception of the Elders who were considerably more equal than everyone else. This was unsettling to me because I knew that the word of God spoke directly against this type of practice.

It was during this summer that a couple of the men in the community that were very opposed to me personally saw me with a Bible in my hand. They immediately brought this to the attention of the Elders. Within a few days I was called into Frank Mosley's office for another one of these interrogation sessions. At which time I was told to go home and get my Bible. Being somewhat naïve I saw this as an opportunity to witness to these people. I went home and got my Bible. At which time they promptly took my Bible away from me. I was also informed at that time that I was too evil to hold a Bible in my hand. That God would never allow me to hold a copy of his Holy Word in my filthy hands. I was also informed that this particular time that I was an undesirable human being by everyone in the community. I was told that no one in the community wanted me around. The only reason I was being tolerated was because I was too young to be excommunicated. I was told that the law of New York State prevented the community from excommunicating and kicking me out completely from their community. This information to me was not exactly new. I had been aware of the fact that I was undesirable in the community for quite some time. I had however found a way to live with that information. The thing that I found so very difficult to live with was the fact that my mother seemed to be going along with the leadership in the community concerning my total undesirable presence. I think also that by this time in my life having come to the understanding that the Lord God favored me for a purpose gave me a great deal of peace. The Holy Spirit also started supernaturally giving me a greater knowledge of the Word of God that I had never acquired through study on my own. The Lord was very definitely protecting me and giving me the ability not only to survive but also to grow in my relationship with my God.

Chapter 20

The Bible And A Vacation In Connecticut

It was towards the end of this summer that the elders of the community decided that the best place for me in the community temporarily was to be with my mother. My mother had gotten the job of cleaning the single man's apartments. These apartments where the single men lived were down by the factory in an old house. This house was two floors and had about five or six men living there. Some of these men were my relatives, my uncles. So for the next few months I assisted my mom in cleaning these single men's living space. During one of these trips to clean the men's living space I started looking around. I was always inquisitive and want to learn more about everything.

One of my uncles did repair on watches for the community. When I went in to look around in his room on the table where he did his watch repair was a small New Testament that had Proverbs and Psalms and it. It was a small brown book with an alligator type cover. I took the New Testament and slipped it into my back pocket. This was a perfect replacement for the Bible that had just been stolen from me by the elders of the community. This little New Testament I could read at night after everyone else was in bed. This small New Testament brought me a great deal of encouragement. It also showed me that a great many of God's people were at all times persecuted. The Psalms especially strengthen me spiritually. Psalms also became a great joy to read.After confessing to my uncle some 30 years later that I had stolen this New Testament from his desk, he told me that he had never had a New Testament like that. He told me then that the only Bible that he ever had was a large black Bible that had been given to him by the Hutterites. This revelation was neat to me because it showed me that the Lord had replaced what the elders of this community had taken away from. This also showed me that I had never been alone in that community. That the Holy Spirit had always accompanied me. The revelation came years later and while it was encouraging, it didn't really help me out too much when I was 11 years old.I was old enough at 11 years to have a fairly good understanding of the word of God. I knew at the time that the way people treated me and looked at me was an indication that they saw something in me that was very different from any of the other children in the community. This difference had far more to do with the persecution that I had encountered it to this point in my life. Everybody in the community was aware of the things that happen to me. I also sensed a protection that was around me. So when I acquired the little New Testament from my uncle'stable I never had any guilty conscience. While I didn't realize it at the time this was a gift from the Lord and I felt comfortable having it. I did not realize it at the time but the favor of God was continually with me. This protection was continually around me and while the Lord's protection did not keep me separated from the persecution it always brought me through the persecution well protected. Again while I did not understand at the time, the persecution was shaping me for what the Lord wants to do with me at a later date. God's protecting hand was also very present with the rest of my family as well.

I also sensed an increased tension and unrest in my mom and dad. I was also well aware that they were fighting their own battles with this community. As Hutterites they had to change their belief system to fit in with Pine Hill. I knew that they were going to have a hard time doing that. My fight with the elders of Pine Hill did not last continually. There were times when I was left alone for months at a time. There were times, sometimes for a couple of months, when I was not called up to the leader's office for interrogation.

It was during this year in late summer and early winter when this community made the purchase of a new place. This new place is located in Norfolk Connecticut. My mother and several other women along with some of the men were selected to go to Norfolk Connecticut to prepare the place for people to move into. I was sent along to be with my mother. The main house on this new place was a stone mansion. Someone very rich had constructed this mansion.

The stone had been imported from European castles that have been ruined. The main dining room in this main building was over 50 feet long and some 30 feet wide. At one end of this dining room were two massive organs. Some 15 feet in from the end wall whare these organs were, was a wall that was made up of black walnut organ pipes.I knew immediately that my job at this place was to explore and check out the entire building. And it was obvious that whoever moved out of this building did not take all of their belongings. In the basement I discovered there was a room that wasabout 10' x 8' that was filled with brass organ pipes. This trip to Norfolk Connecticut community lasted about two weeks. Towards the end of the second week and a few days before leaving to go back to Pine Hill I made an incredible discovery. While exploring in one of the rooms in the basement of the main building I found an interesting small statuette. I came across this discovery of the statuette quite by accident. It was in a room that was filled with a lot of debris, canning jars and empty boxes. Behind some canning jars, and some boxes, I located an object that had been wrapped in soft cloth.After making sure that there was nobody watching me and there was no one near me in the basement I picked the object up. I again made sure that I was the only one in the basement because I didn't want anyone to see what I'd found. I unwrapped this object. Inside the cloth wrapped up multiple times was a small statuette. It appeared to be a carving. This carving was made out of white stone that at first I thought was clouded quartz. The stone however was brilliantly white and had a slightly perlled affect to it. This stone was something special. The carving was of a mountain sheep laying down facing straight forward. The carving was a little bit over 4 inches long about 2 ½ almost 3 inches wide and about 3 1/2 inches high. It felt like it weighs about a pound and a half. I was not about to let this carving fall into the wrong hands. How could I hide this little carving so nobody would know that I had it.I came up with a plan. I purposely left something that I'd brought with me to Connecticut in the basement. I placed the carving in a secure place near the stairway. I also knew that within a few days we would be going back to New York. The plan I had was quite simple. When everyone was ready to leave just before the doors of the building were locked I would run back downstairs to retrieve an object I had left there. Along with retrieving my personal belonging I would also take the statuette. But I wasn't sure yet how was going to hide it in the car going back to New York. I knew that I would come up with a plan. When time came to go, the first part of my plan worked beautifully. I was even allowed with no supervision to run down in the basement and get my personal belongings. When I got the mountain sheep I had already wrapped it in a soft cloth I found it in. I took the mountain sheep statuette and put it in my pants. When I walked with my hand in my right pocket it concealed what I had hid. I kept this statuette of the mountain sheep hidden until I was forced to leave the community when I was 13 ½ years old. I had no idea of the value of this little mountain sheep statuette but I knew that this was not a piece of junk. It would not be until many years later that I would actually discover its value.

The time that I got to spend a Connecticut was a wonderful vacation. At times spent away from the prying eyes of management at Pine Hill. And while I was required to work in Connecticut to work was not demanding. I got considerable amount of time away from everyone to be on my own. The trip back to New York state was almost uneventful. I had only been back at Pine Hill for a few hours when the harsh reality of my existence came rushing back to me. I was informed on that same day that my separation from the rest of the children in the community would have to continue. While I was not required to work in the shop full-time I would have to be separated from the rest of the children.

Chapter 21

Solitary And Slave Labor

By this time school had already started. I had attended school for the last half of September and the first half of October. The weather had been extremely warm for this time of year. I was wearing only a pair of shorts and a T-shirt. My brothers and I came home to the house on Friday afternoon. My mother seemed a little bit upset that we didn't understand why.Because we weren't sure whether this had anything to do with us or not we made ourselves scarce. Within an hour afterwe came home two men showed up at the door.The elders of the community had sent these men to our door. Both of these menwere members of the community and had been around for quite a while. When my mother called for me, I came to find out what she wanted. Without saying a word to me she took me to where the men were sitting in the living room. The men each grabbed one of my hands and they led me away. Neither one of them said a single word to me. I also realized that it was no use struggling to try to free myself. After asking them several times where they were taking me and not receiving an answer I decided the best thing to do is to keep my mouth shut. I was taken across the community to ahouse that was very near the building that housed the laundry. They took me into this building we walked up the stairs to the fourth floor. They came to a room that had a locked door.They unlocked the door with a key. They put me into this room locked the door and I heard them leave. This room was about 8' x 10'. There was a table, a chair by the table, and a bunk bed. On the bunk bed were a mattress and a pill. There were no sheets, no blankets, and no pillowcases. There was a light fixture in the ceiling, but no light bulb. I had no clue what was going on, or why I had been locked into this room. Again this defies all reason, and logic, and Christian principle. I stayed in this room all night. This was the third week in October. Temperatures at night went below freezing. When no one showed up at the room to get me out, it occurred to me that I would be here for a considerable period of time. No one showed up that evening with anything for me to eat. No one even showed up to see if I needed to go to the bathroom. When the room got dark that evening I tried to sleep. That is when I discovered there was also no heat in this room. As I stated before the only thing I was wearing was a pair of shorts and a T-shirt. There was no way for me to keep warm. I shivered so hard that the bed continues shook and rattled against the wall. After several hours of listening to the sound of the bed rattling I finally got out of bed and pulled the bed away from the wall. Sleep was still nearly impossible to come by. I finally realized that if I curled up on one end of the mattress I could fold the mattress over and cover myself with it. But this method of covering myself to keep warm made little difference.

This confinement upset me greatly. As much as I thought about what had gone wrong I could find no reason why I should be locked up in this manner. What in the world had I done that was so evil that prompted my mother to betray me and called the elders of the community and have me locked up.When left alone for any length of time the human mind wanders. I was not yet 12 years old. My mind for sure wandered. No one came to the door until the next morning at about nine o'clock. Of course I judge time by the light of the sunrise. When someone finally showed up at the door it was an older woman. She brought in a tray with some food on it. I desperately needed to go to bathroom and after pleading with her she finally let me go. But she watched me very closely all the time. I tried to ask her why I'd been locked up but she said nothing. She would not give me any more information about anything. She may very well not have known anything. The elders of the community will quite often keep Information like this to themselves. I also asked this older woman if I could have a blanket. Again she said nothing but turned around and left the room making sure that the door was locked. I was very happy however to receive the food. I sat down and started to eat. The food that I'd been served was overcooked, cold, and hard oatmeal, toaster that had been burnt black, and milk that I knew had been on the kitchen table overnight. The milk did not smell very good. I was starved because I didn't have any dinner the night before. I ate the food and was very happy to have it.

I didn't see anyone or hear from anyone the entire day. At eight o'clock that evening, an older woman showed up again, with a tray of food.Again I was allowed to go to the bathroom. Again when I question the woman to try to find out some information about my confinement I was told nothing. Again I ask this woman if I could have a blanket because there was no heat in the room. Again she left and locked the door without saying anything. The food this time was a little more nutritious. It was stew that had been cooked for dinner that was served to the adults at six o'clock that evening. This Stew however had two hours to cool off. This stew was not only cold but had a half-inch of greece on top of it. By this time the cold food with grease on it did not make much difference.I ate the food because I was hungry and I was very thankful to have it. By this time in my experience with this community and with the elders I knew a little bit about their method of treating severely defective convicts like myself. I knew that there was some hellacious crime that I had committed. But if I had committed this crime I must have been sleepwalking because I had no knowledge of it. For the life of me I could not come up with a reason why my mother would do this to me. Except of course it was a wonderful way for her to dispose of me. I started doing the only thing that I knew how. There was no paper notepad or pencil there was absolutely nothing in this room. The only thing left for me to do was to pray.For the next 10 days I spent most of my waking hours crying out to the Lord. I knew that God answered prayer so I knew that sooner or later I would hear from Him. My cry to Lord was, your word says that you would never leave or forsake us. Why is it that you have left me in this hellhole alone? A room with a locked door. What have I done that has been so evil that has caused you to totally withdraw from the. Why is it that I cannot cens yourpresents? After the fifth or sixth day I started contemplating how I could bring about the end of my life. In a 3 ½ years I had been in this community I had been mistreated more than any living human being has a right to. I felt that my brothers and I had suffered far worse than all of the other kids in this community combined. I was just at the end of my hope and I felt, the end of my purpose. What could God possibly want with somebody like me? If I was really as evil and as demonic and as full of the devil as these people said I was then surely I had no right to live. I started praying earnestly with tears and hopelessness that the Lord would allow me to end my life. All of my prayers seemingly went unanswered. That is until the 10th day.

It was one or two o'clock in the morning on the 10th day someone call my name. The first time I heard my name called I did not answer. I really felt that if someone was at the door they would have to open it and come in and see if I was really alive. After a few minutes my name was called again. This time I looked around to see if there's anyone in the room, or if somebody was out side the door. There was no one there. Again a third time my name was called. This time I asked who is it that's calling my name. Again I heard a voice, it said "I have not left you nor have I forsaken you. If you will be of good courage and be strong I will lead you out of here". The voice that spoke with me was the most beautiful sound I have ever heard. The voice was filled with love and kindness. I also sent deep in my spirit that whoever the voice belonged to really cared for me. My answer to this was "all I want to do is die and to go home to be with my Lord". The voice answered and said "no I will not do that. I will raise you up to serve me someday". I said "Lord if you are going to force me to live, then I want to live only to serve you from this day forward because there is nothing in this world that I want. My spirit and my heart at this point are completely broken". In less than 10 minutes the Lord showed me what this covenant that I was entered into with Him really meant.What it would mean for a lifetime commitment to serve Him. I said "Lord this is what I really want to do". The Lord said to me "I will never ever leave you I will always be with you. You will never be alone". This entire conversation that I had with the Lord Jesus I heard with my ears. Though I did not see him physically with my eyes his presence and his glory fill that room. When the conversation was over I knew that He had not left. The other thing that I experienced instantly was that my body warmed up like somebody had drawn an electric blanket over me. For the rest of the time of solitary confinement I never spent another cold night. The presence of the Lord Jesus was so prevalent in the room that I was never cold again. There was also a joy and peace that sprang up in me that I could not understand. When the older woman who brought my food the next morning opened the door, I greeted her with so much joy in my spirit that she dropped a tray of food on the floor. And she left very hurriedly and forgot to lock the door. I took this opportunity to go to bathroom and take a nice long hot shower. Nobody came to bother me. In fact I did not see anyone until about eight o'clock that evening.My confinement was to last another 20 days. But it was 20 days that I spent in the presence of God. The glory of God never left that room. His presence was so powerful that I never had another unhappy moment in that room alone. The favor of God had been so powerfully present in that room that I could almost touch it with my hands. The Holy Spirit was with me from that point on and far more powerfully. God was definitely preparing me for something. I knew from this moment on that these people could not bring me any harm. My Outlook on life changed dramatically from this moment forward. The joy and peace that I had experienced that night never again left me. Every time from this moment on when anxiety and uncertainty about my situation grabbed my spirit the Lord always brought me peace and joy.

A man named Jack Mason knew me and favored me to a degree. He went to work to try to have me released from solitary confinement. Within a few days his efforts paid off. He came in one morning and told me that I'd been released into his and his wife's care. This young couple has a daughter that was about five years old. The little girl had known me from around the community. I always got along well with her. But now it seemed like I had made a brand-new friend. This little girl must have sensed the pain that had becomes so much a part of my daily routine. But I think that she also sensed a joy that was now very present in me. Younger children are quite often very sensitive to things like this in people. The man and his wife had set up a room in their home for me. While I was alone in this room and the door was closed at night it was never locked. I was assured that I would have access to the bathroom and also to take a shower when I needed to. While in solitary confinement I only got to take a shower twice. I was also informed that the next morning I would have to go to work in a factory. But I would have no more access to any of the other children in the community. I could not contact my mother or father or any of my brothers or sisters in any way. In fact I was not permitted to talk or communicate with anyone.

The next morning I was taken down to the factory. The manager of the factory was a middle-aged man whose children I knew from the community. I also was familiar with the manager of the factory. This man was familiar with my situation. But it seemed to make very little difference that I was only 12 years old. I was expected to do a man's work every single day. I was also required to work any overtime that the rest of the men worked. I was to do my work without any unnecessary communication with any other living human being. I also discovered a lot of the men in the factory took considerable advantage of me. The abuse also did not diminish in any degree. The equipment that I was required to work on was woodworking equipment. Woodworking equipment can be extremely noisy and can severely damage your hearing. When I got an opportunity to go to the bathroom for a few minutes, I got some toilet paper and put it in my ears. This offends the noise so that my ears did not hurt. This lasted for about 2 ½ or three hours. One of the men saw me with toilet paper in my ears and came up to me and pulled it out. He told me that I would have to work without any earplugs because this was a part of my punishment. I had still to this point never been told what it was I was being punished for.

One of the first jobs that I had in his factory was to work on a planar. A man set the planar to plain off about 1/16 of an inch of wood off the surface of some boards. After he set the planar he started to feed the wood through. It was my job to catch the wood as it came out of the machine. I was to stack the boards neatly on a wagon. These boards that we were planning had to be run through the machine five times. While the man was resetting the machine for another cut I excused myself and again went to the bathroom. Again put toilet paper in my ears. But this time I also stuffed a bunch of toilet paper in my pocket.Again I was on the receiving end of the machine taking the boards and stacking them neatly on the wagon. Another man came up to me and saw the toilet paper in my ears, and again pulled the toilet paper out. Again I was told that this was a part of my punishment.

This whole setup was a conspiracy that everyone in the community knew about except me. As soon as this man turned his back to walk away I inserted more hearing protection in my ears. The man, who was operating the machine, decided that I was standing around too much. So he started speeding up the amount of wood that was coming through the machine ata time. The wood came through so fast that I could not stack it anymore. So I sat down in the corner by the wall and watch the wood fall on the floor.When he was finished he came around the machine and saw the pile of wood on the floor and informed me that I was going to have to pick it up. At which point I very quickly excused myself and ran to the bathroom in an emergency. I stayed away just long enough for this man to pick up the wood himself.I soon discovered that there was more than one way to play this silly game that they were playing. If I was going to be punished for doing something I knew nothing about, then I was going to enjoy some of the time and punishment. Besides I was not stupid I'd been abused in this community before and I had been able to perceive the weaknesses in people. I learned how to use these weaknesses against them. So again I started watching and listening to these people very carefully. I soon discovered that most of these people only believe in Christian principles as long as they benefited themselves and their families. But when they had to extend the Christian principles to other people they were not Christians anymore. So I started playing by their rules. I soon discovered that most of the time the men that had me working under them walked away from me angry. Now I knew the rules of the game. I learned how to play it very well and more often than not I won. It was during this time of slave labor in their factory that I started to lose my hearing. The story of the healing of my hearing will be told in later chapter. This slave labor was to continue for almost a year.The man that I was working with on the planar, seemed to be fairly easy-going. I asked him if there was any chance that I could feed the wood into the planar. He could take the wood at the other end and stack it on the wagon. He quite readily agreed. I think he expected me to get into trouble. He set up the planar for the next cut. At first I started putting the boards in nice and slow and he kept up with stacking them quite nicely. But after about five or six minutes of this I started feeding the boards in just as fast as I could. I worked a whole load of boards on the wagon just that fast. When I was finished I shut the machine off. I came around the machine and saw that he was still picking up wood off the floor.He had about half of the wood still to pick up. I said to him that I was very surprised that he couldn't keep up. After all it's a simple job just to stack wood from the machine onto a wagon. He got very angry with me at which point I excused myself and went to the men's room.This man very quickly learned that I had very little to lose by being rebellious, having a wrong attitude, or being downright disobedient. After all what else could this community do to me. Hangings in the town square had been outlawed for a considerable number of years.After all if they were Christian they would notthink of abusing me. After the first couple of days working in the factory it became quite apparent to most of the men that I really didn't care very much anymore. If they were going to abuse me to very quickly discovered that they were abuses that I have my own that I could give back to them. It did not take very long however for this information to spread to the elders of the community. I was again called up to the office for another round of interrogating counseling. It was at this point that I came to a full understanding of what the Lord meant when he told me that he would never leave me. His presence and an increased protection that he had put around me was very much seen and felt.

Some of the other jobs that I was asked to do was to run a small shaper. This small shaper was set up to cut the sharp edges off the ends of play blocks that they made. This was a relatively easy job. However on a number of occasions when the man was setting up this job he seemed a little bit confused. So when he would walk away from the machine for a few minutes I went ahead and finish setting the job up. This seemed to make him quite angry. Apparently I had accomplished something that he was unable to finish at the time. Another job that I was asked to do frequently was to cut these play blocks to the proper length. This was done on a large radial arm saw. This particular radial arm saw was the Type with thehead of the machine that contained the cutting blade was suspended from an overhead bracket. This saw swung straight out towards the operator. This was quite a dangerous piece of equipment. Another job that I was asked to do from time to time, was to feed wood into the end of a large molding machine. This machine would shape all four sides of a particular piece of wood as the wood was pushed through the machine by a series of steel rollers. This again was a very dangerous machine to operate. I had been at this factory in slave labor for three or four weeks. I had been allowed to operate some extremely dangerous machinery. The thought occurred to me maybe these people were allowing me to operate this dangerous equipment for the sole purpose of causing an injury there were severe enough to kill. This thought seemed a little bit ludicrous at the time. As time went on however and I were still required to operate this very dangerous equipment that thought only strengthened.

While working in this factory as a slave employee I was never permitted casual conversation with anyone else that worked in this factory. Lunch breaks and coffee breaks I was forced to take by myself. I discovered that if I am going to take these lunch breaks by myself I could busy myself by going exploring. The shop that we worked in was located at the edge of the woods. I found myself spending more and more time walking in the woods. This got me away from the angry looks of the other men in the shop. They were treating me more and more as though I had some strange contagious disfiguring disease. They made it very obvious to me that I was an undesirable human being. Whenever they came towards me they made a very intentional and deliberate effort to walk around. If I did ever attempt to talk to them they pretended not to hear me or just simply ignored me. My father's uncle worked in this factory as well. He put a word in with management of this factory on my behalf. After that I started spending more and more time working with him. He at least didn't treat me as an undesirable alien.

My work in this factory for the next 11 months actually went quite well. Some of the manI treated the same way that they treated me, complained to the elders. I very soon found out that this was going to get me into more trouble. Here again how much more trouble could I get into. They couldn't do any worse to me than what they were already doing. But I tried in every situation to first of all find grounds to communicate verbally with the people that were doing the wrong. If there was no other way to handle the situation then I resorted to defensive measures. Every single time I treated one of these men as badly as they treated me, they ran to the elders or the supervisor of the shop and complained. It was kind of interesting to me that these full-grown men couldn't even take from a 12-year-old boy what they were dishing out to him. Their Christianity didn't even seem to be skin deep.

During this 11 month of forced labor I very seldom saw my father or my two younger brothers. They were fighting their own battles in their own way. It was during this period of time when I was in slave labor in a factory that the community decided to build a new shop. In the process of building the shop my dad was helping a few other men hang some large steel doors. These doors are large enough when opened to allow a truck to back into the building. One of these doors in the process of being hung slipped and fell on my father's foot. Very nearly cutting my father foot and half. I found out about his injury inadvertently. Everyone was trying to keep it a secret from me. I made an effort to go see my dad. Whom I managed to see for about a half hour. One of the elders of the community saw me and came and grabbed hold of me and drags me away. These people really enjoy seeing someone suffer to the max.

The 11 months of slave labor finally came to an end. I was allowed to go back home with my parents and the rest of my family. I was slowly over another couple of months reintegrated into the school system. By this time everyone in the community knew that I was totally evil and that they had to avoid me and stay completely away from me. That year in school they advanced me from sixth grade to eighth grade. It was a very difficult move for me because by this time I was having serious psychological problems. The peace and joy that the Lord had istilled in my spirit was always with me. The healing for my serious psychological problems he paid me for the time being at least. It was however enough to know without any doubt that the Lord was continually present with me

Chapter 22

Excommunication On The Farm

That next summer in early May my father took me to Kingston New York to the Social Security office. We went into the office and the girl that waited on us at the counter started processing my application for a Social Security number. When I asked her what the Social Security number was for, she explained the system to me. I told the girl that I would never live long enough to collect Social Security. The girl processed the paperwork and issued me a number. On the way home I could see that my father was visibly troubled. When we got home he went down to the shoe shop and asked me to come with him. I guess he remembered what had been happen to me for the last year. The solitary confinement of a month and 11 months in slave labor. He was visibly upset. He asked me how I knew that I would never collect Social Security. I told my dad that I knew how I was going to die. When he asked how I was going to die. I told him that I was going to be shot through the heart with a high-powered rifle. But I assured him that this would not happen until I was an old man. When he asked me how I knew all this I told him that I wasn't sure. "I know a lot of stuff that's going to happen in the future but I don't know how I know".I told him that it was the same thing when one of the kids got hurt I could feel their physical pain. Like the girl the winter before that had broken her collarbone.Untilthey got her to the hospital and set the bone my collarbone hurt just as bad as hers did.It was nothing personal, I just had discovered over the past couple of years that whenever somebody around me got hurt I experienced their physical pain. This was another very good reason to stay away from most people. My father never pursued this to find out more about what I was seeing or experiencing. But I saw that he was visibly troubled by what was going on with me. I assured him that I was not about to kill myself. That seamed to ease his minds a little bit.

By the end of May I discovered why I needed a Social Security number. The elders of the community had gotten me a job on a farm about 35 or 40 miles away. In the last week of May I was taken to this farm and introduced to the farmer I was to work for. It had all be prearranged. I was to work for board and room, and personal necessities. I was not to receive any money as pay. The farmer and his wife were wonderful people. At first it was very difficult to live with somebody I didn't know and work in a place I had never before been to. But I very quickly discovered that the farmer and his wife were very kind loving people. They treated me as if I was their own son. I lived in the house with them and had my own room. This farmer had another hired hand working for him who was an older man in his late 50s. The two of us very quickly became good friends. Working like this for people who didn't know me gave me a chance to prove myself. I found out quite quickly that what the community elders had told this man about me did not prove to be true. The farmer and his wife also discovered that most of the rumors and information that they had gotten about me from the community was totally different than what I prove to be. He quickly discovered that when I was given instructions as to what to do that I carried out my duties honestly and to the best of my ability. The work that I was given to do was always done well. The man was so impressed with the work that I did that he soon started to inquirer about the circumstances of my being kicked out of the community. It was also through the kindness of this farmer and his wife that I finally had somebody around me that cared enough to show me how to overcome my handicaps. At meal times this man and his wife went through great lengths and effort to teach me how to eat properly without spilling food all over. The trembling in my hands did not totally disappear. I learned how to compensate for handicaps in social environments. This summer working for this couple was a gift from God. Unknowingly the elders in this community had given me exactly what I needed for the future. The elders in the community were making every effort now and had made every effort in the past to continue to dominate my life in every way possible. This job on the farm was also a continue effort to dispose of me permanently one way or another. However with this particular job they gave me an opportunity to learn how to integrate into society at large. This older couple that I worked for was a godsend. With the interest that they took in me and the counseling that I received from them was totally amazing.The farmer and his wife both explained to me that they werenot doing this to find fault with me. But that they were doing this for me to help to undo the damage that had been done in the past. We spent considerable hoursin the evenings talking about some of the things that had happen to me in the community. The man also soon discovered that I had skills that he could use on his farm because I had grown up on a farm in North Dakota. I soon learned how to milk cows and how to do other chores on a dairy farm that I had never done before.He also allowed me to drive tractors to do other work around the farm. The care and attention that I received from this couple was far superior to any pay you could have given me with money. The only problem with the job was it only lasted three months. The other man that worked on this farm also took a liking to me. He treated me as an equal and more importantly as a friend. I also learned a great deal from him. And he was also very instrumental in bringing about a degree of stability in me.

Towards the end of the first week in September my father came to the farm to take me back to the community. I talked with my dad in every way I could to stay where I was. But it was no use the farmer would love to have mestay. The hired man told me when I left that if I ever needed a place to go to, that I should come and see him at the farm. That he would be very willing to help me out. I had finally made some friends that had really made a positive difference in my life.

Chapter 23

Complete Excommunication

At the beginning of this school year I was to start high school. This meant walking to the bottom of the driveway which was about a mile long to catch the bus to go to Kingston New York to the local high school. Going to high school in Kingston New York for me was an incredible experience. There were so many other kids that had similar problems to what I had experienced in my life that I got along quite well. Getting along with other kids in high school was not a problem. In fact the ones I got along with the best were African-Americans. This was the school year of 1960 and 1961. Segregation was very much in effect in the minds and hearts of people both black and white. On the school bus the black kids sat in the seats that white kids did not want to sit in. This was not always at the back of the bus. The back of the bus was reserved for the guys and their girlfriends to make out. But the black kids were mistreated in general just about as badly as I had been in the Christian community. This first year of high school I got along quite well. I discovered that in the school system there was a guidance counseling office. When I was in a situation where things bothered me beyond my ability to cope with there was always someone in this guidance counseling office that was willing to listen. Some of the teachers that I had were also very helpful.

In my first year in high school I did quite well in all my subjects mostly C's and B's. But English was a disaster. To me it was still a foreign language. I could speak English but I did not know English. It was very difficult for me to gain comprehensive knowledge of English. Going to high school was one of the best things that happened to me. Because it gave me a chance to be away from the community and all of the people that were looking for opportunities to knock my legs out from under me.It almost put to an end to the interrogation sessions that I had endured for over three years inthe leaders office. By associating with other kids in Kingston high school I soon discovered that I was not the only one with problems. I discovered that some of these kids came from extremely poor backgrounds. Although their problems were somewhat different than mine, a lot of them were almost as disfunctional as I was. Therewere also times with other kids, when serious conflict came up between us. But in every situation I found out that our problems could be worked out between ourselves. This experience of high school also was very import because it prepared me for the next step in my life. The next step of my life was to be brought on me much sooner than I had anticipated.

The next attack came not only against me but also against my whole family. By this time my family consisted of 12 children. This next move against our family I never saw coming. It occurred in early spring of 1961. We were just coming home from school in Kingston. We arrived home at about 3:30 in the afternoon. As we got to our house we saw that our entire family was already seated in a large station wagon. My two older sisters and myself were told, as we came up to the car that we would have to get into the car. When I inquired where we were going I was told that we are being asked to leave the community. I question my mother further and wanted to know why. But she did not give me an answer. I gave my schoolbooks to one of my sisters. I told my father who was driving the car to stay here at the house and to wait for me to return. I asked them please not to follow me. There was something that I had to take care of on my own.I went to the main building in the community, which housed the offices of the leader, and the second in command. The second-in-command was the only one in the office. I walked into his office and stood in front of his desk and demanded to know why my family was being forced to leave the community. He looked me right in the eyes and told me that why my family is being asked to leave is none of my business. That if I did not know why I am being asked to leave he was not going to tell me. All I am going to tell you he said is that you are never ever permitted to come back here. I looked him right in the eyes and I told him that the pain and suffering that he had imposed on myself and my mother and father was not only not christian, but was uncalled for and that from that moment on I would consider it brutal and abusive treatment. I would also consider the way I've been treated for the last four years nothing short of persecution.I also informed him that the leadership of this community had no idea how to live the Christian life. I told him that the way we had been treated as a family for the last four years totally defied all of the teachings in the Bible.

I went back to where my father and mother and family were waiting for me in the car. I walked up to my dad and told him to wait for a few more minutes there was something I had to get. I ran up in the woods where I had hidden the carving of the mountain sheep that was carved out of a white stone.I retrieved it so that I could keep it with me. When I got back to the car my father and mother wanted to know what I went in the woods for. I simply told them that I have hidden something in the woods I want to have and keep. As my father drove our family to the place we would be living, it was a quiet and somber ride. We were being moved to a house that was not very far away from the community. My father needed to find a job, which he had not yet found. There had however been a job found for myself. My father said that the next morning he would take me up to the place where I was going to work and live. It was a farm up near Binghamton New York. I was being kicked out of community and it was necessary that I go to live on my own and work on a farm a long ways away for my family as well.

This experience with being excommunicated as a family unit showed me the true nature of this so-called Christian community. In many aspects of this community's lifestyle, they were anything but Christian. I had begun to realize as long as two years earlier that my entire family were suffering unusually harsh treatment at the hands of the Elders of this community. Our family had found it difficult to leave behind the ways that we had learned what the Hutterites. Our lack of ability to decode and convert to a completely new way of life have caused us a great deal of trouble. The thing that was so troubling to me was that the Hutterites were a Christian community. Why was it necessary for us to convert from the Christian principles that we had been living under with the Hutterites.

Chapter 24

The Farmer Family

This farm was in a very rural area near asmall town of Calacoon New York. A family owned this farm by the name of Johnson. Josephine the wife and mother of thisfamily greeted me fairly warmly. I was shown to a room that would the mybedroom. This room was on the first floor just off the kitchen. It already had one occupant. The occupant was an older man by the name of Joe. Joe was not quite right mentally. But he was a fairly personable man and quite easy to get along with most of the time. The oldest daughter in this family was named Darlene. Darlene had recently turned 18. Now she was a full-grown woman with rights of her own and she didn't mind letting everyone know that. When I first met Darlene I knew that I did not want to have a fight with her. She was a strong girl and stood exactly six-foot tall. She was also very nice to me and treated me with respect and I knew I was going to like her. The second oldest daughter's name was Jennifer. She did herwork around the farm very well. From the very beginning she also treated me with respect. But Jennifer was going to make me prove myself in every way at every point. She was one of those girls that didn't cut a man very much slack. Jennifer was going to be a challenge. But I soon found out that she had respect for someone who could stand his or her ground. The father's name was Simon. He was a large man and stood at just about 6 foot tall. He weighed just less than 300 pounds. But he was a very muscular man. And it was obvious from the very beginning that his word was law. This was his farm and his family and things were going to be done his way. The oldest son's name was George. Little George had an attitude from the very beginning. He was one of those boys that wanted to get in your face and make you be the one to back up. George was two years younger than me. George was also over 30 pounds lighter than myself. I knew from the beginning that I had the advantage over him. There were two other younger boys; one was Carl and the other wasMickey. I could see from the beginning that this family was going to be fun to live with and work with.George, however I was going to have problems with.From the very beginning he was out to force me to prove that I was a man and could stand my ground in a fight. George pushed the limit every time he had any opportunity or excuse todoso. Carl was not much of a problem, he was all mouth. Jennifer treated me better than anyone else in the family. Jennifer was one year older than myself and she was also one grade ahead of me in high school. When no one else saw what Jennifer was doing she was even helpful to me. It seemed like Jennifer did not want anyone else to know that she was being nice to me. I could live with that. Her attitude seemed to be, don't make any advances on me and I'll treat you with respect. The mother Josephine was very compassionate from the very beginning.It was quite obvious to me that whoever had secured this job for me had already told these people quite a bit about me. About an hour after my arrival I got to meet the father and the owner of his farm Simon Peters. He was a man that was very much up front and wanted everybody to know that he was totally in control. Not much was going to get done without his personal approval. I liked him from the very beginning because he let me know exactly where I stood. From the very first day he let me know exactly what my responsibilities were going to be and the work that I was going to be expected to do. As long as I did my work and didn't get in his way or cause any problems in the family, I was cut a lot of slack.

When he got me alone on the first day, he told me that when I was working for him in summer he would give me $100 a month and board and room. In winter when I was going to school he would give me $25 a month and board and room. I would have to be responsible for buying my own clothes and school supplies and anything else that I need. It was a kind of understood with him from the beginning that I would have to make my own way. I really like that. For once in my life I had some say as to what was going to happen to me from day to day. It also told me that for the first time in my life I would have some control over what I did and how I did it. The entire family seems to be quite a normal family. The sibling rivalry was very real. Also to a degree there was a spirit of mild rebellion against the father. The father was quite heavy-handed in his authority over his children and his wife. Everything and everybody in Simon Peters life worked exactly the way he wanted it to or he made necessary corrections. This included people as well as machinery or animals.

After sayinggoodbye to my father I brought my personal belongings into my bedroom. I was not to see my father again or anyone else in my family for almost 2 years. Simon took me down to the barn. He explain to me what he expected of me. I was to do the milking of the dairy cows in the morning and in the evening. I was to be up every morning at 4:30 AM. Milking at night started at 4:00 PM. I was to do the milking six days a week. I would get sunday off. During the rest of the day when I was not in school, I would be required to help around the farm with any work that needed to be done. This also meant operating equipment in a proper fashion. My schedule started the very next morning. I knew from the beginning that living on this farm and working for this man was going to be a challenge. But I also understood that I was going to have to prove myself to everyone in this family. But as I proved myself I was also going to be extended respect for which I was grateful. Georges relationship with me from the beginning was going to be confrontational. George was a young boy who was trying hard to grow up. But at every step of the way at every moment of the day he had to prove that he is stronger faster and better than somebody that he considered his opponent. I was considered by him to be his opponent.

We arrived at this farm at about 10 o'clock in the morning. Lunch was served shortly after noon. I had lunch with these people and from the beginning I got along with everyone very well. Darlene called me out on every single characteristic in me that she didn't think quite measured up to her standards. She was very cynical and very critical. But since I was very young I had developed a sense of humor. My sense of humor in most cases would save the day in my relationship with Darlene. In heart and spirit she was quite a soft loving and understanding human being. Jennifer was the one in the family who kept me on my toes. But Jennifer'srelationship with me was not one of confrontation. She was much more encouraging and persuasive in a very nice way. She had no interest in scoring any points with me. I think from the beginning Jennifer saw that I had some personal problems, and she was very willing to help me overcome them. Jennifer never made any attempt to make my personal problems a public spectacle. Jennifer appeared to be very sensitive and kind. But she did not want those traits to be too clearly seen by to many people.

It was already June, and crops had already been planted in the fields. It was a time between the planting of crops and waiting for the hay to be tall enough to cut. From the start Simon wanted to know if I was any good at repairing machinery. I had a very good mechanical aptitude and I adapted to repairing machinery very well. Growing up with my family I had used hand tools many times. I had a very good imagination and a desire to learn more. That first afternoon I was to be put to the test, because there was machinery that needed to be repaired. Simon showed me the machinery and told me what repairs needed to be made. He made some instructions and suggestions on how he thought that I should do those repairs. Then he left me alone to do what he instructed me to do. A couple of hours later when he came back the repairs had been done properly. This impressed Simon. At four o'clock in the afternoon milking of the dairy cows started. This farm had 125 cows to milk twice a day. The main barn held 100 animals; the scond held barn 25 animals. Milking the dairy cows was also not much of a challenge because this is work that I had done before. The summer before this I had worked on a farm for 2 ½ months. It was during that summer that I learned how to operate milking machines. I was also quite good around animals. The equipment that I used were four double milking machines. I also found out that I was not expected to run all four of these machines alone. Jennifer was always there to help me out and make sure things run properly. She was unofficially left in charge when her father was not there. This arrangement brought considerable frustration to George. As the oldest son in the family he felt that it was his responsibility to be totally in charge of everything when his father was not around. I was very pleased to see that Jennifer ran things.

I really enjoyed working and living with his family. I had support from Jennifer on most occasions. Confrontational challenges came from George. In the two years that I was on this farm George never stopped looking for an opportunity to have a physical confrontation with me. Darlene never really got in my way. By that fall she had moved out to attend school to become an airline stewardess. The one that was going to post the most challenge to me was Simon. When things didn't go his way he had a considerable temper, and he had a tendency to lash out at the first person that was near him. That quite often was me. While he never actually hit me he came close a few times. But I was fast enough on my feet to get out of the way. And as a large man he didn't move very fast. But I discovered that being nimble and getting out of his way showed him that I could take care of myself. As time went on I gained a considerable amount of respect in Simon's eyes. From beginning I grew into this family very well. While I was let know more in body language then words, that I was an outsider, I was still accepted as one of the family. Josephine liked me from the start. She treated me like one of her own sons. I do not think that she ever made any distinction between her own children and myself. She just accepted me that way from the beginning. But she also expected me to carry my share of the responsibilities around the house. I never had any problem doing extra for her because she treated me better than anyone else in the family. She was also the best cook I had ever seen in my life. I always went out of my way to try to do extra for her that would be helpful. This kind of cemented our relationship from the start.

By the second week in July we were out in the field cutting hay. I was given responsibility for cutting the hay. I was driving a small Massey Ferguson tractor that had a six-foot cycle bar mower. This job would put me alone for a good part of the day. That I really enjoyed. I could spend time working out problems, and spent time in prayer. I never wanted to forget that the Lord had protected me this far and that he was always with me. The Lord alone was the reason that I had survived this far. The other wonderful thing about spending time alone cutting hay was the wildlife that I saw. It is quite apparent from the very beginning working in the fields that the deer population in this part of New York was quite extensive. Deer liked having their fawns in the hayfields. The young fawns were very reluctant to move out of the way of the morning machine. That meant that I had to pay very close attention to what I was doing. At all times I had to keep my eyes open for fawns in front of the tractor or front of the mowing machine.

The hey was allowed to dry for three days until the moisture level was low enough so that the hay would not heat up to much in a mow. Then the hay would be bailed. When the bailing started I was expected to be there to help pick bails up off the ground. The bales were stacked on four-wheeled wagon six or seven tiers high. We loaded two wagons at a time. These wagons were then pulled with the tractor to the barn. They were unloaded one at a time onto an elevator that took the bales one at a time up into the haymow. One of us was at the bottom placing the hay bales on the elevator. The rest of us were up in a haymow stacking the bales in place. The baleshad to be stacked neatly so that a man could walk on top of each layer without falling in a hole. This also allowed maximum number of bales to be placed in thehaymow.

Mowing hay, bailing hay,and picking hay up off the ground was going to beheavy work. I needed to have my physique built up. While I was born and raised on a farm my time spent with this cult did not involve very much physical labor. Besides if I was going to stand up against the aggressive challenge of George I was going to have to start muscling out. Mostdays mowing hay were also quite long. My day started at 4:30 AM and ended at eight or nine o'clock at night. We always came into the house at 7 AM or 7:30 AM for breakfast. Every day at about noon we stopped for lunch. Lunch was served in the kitchen if we were around the house. If we were out in the field, Josephine brought lunch out to us. On days that we were bailing hay Josephine drove the tractor that pulled the Baylor. I really enjoyed working with these people because everyone in the family took part in making this farm work. Even the younger children Carl and Mickey were there to lend a hand. I got along very well with Carl and Mickey because they were at the stage of growing up in development that I had been at just a few years ago.

Old Joe at the time I knew him must have been in his late 50s or early 60s. He was a man of medium build about 5'6" tall. I would guess his weight probably 175 pounds. For a man of his age he could handle himself extremely well. He did chores mainly around the barn. But when we were picking up hay, Joe was always there to help. He always brought along his pitchfork. He would pick up a bale of hay with the pitchfork and put it up six tears on wagon. The bales weighed about 35 or 40 pounds. When Joe became angry with anyone he was also very good at throwing a pitchfork. He coulde throw a pitchfork as good as any man could throw a spear. When Joe threw the pitchfork and it hit a wood post or a wall it always stuk. So I knew that I did not want to become a target of Joe's thrown pitchfork. Joe had his weird ways about him but was fairly easy to get along with. I would guess that his IQ was about that of a 10-year-old boy. But Joe was very conscientious about doing his full share of the work and doing it right.

Starting about the middle or the end of September we started to cut corn. Corn was cut in the field by a corn chopper was pulled by one tractor to the silo. The corn was cutinto pieces about the size of wood chips so that the cows could eat it properly. Another tractor drove behind a corn chopper and slightly to the left side pulling a wagon that the chopped corn was blown into. The wagonloads of corn would then be taken to the barn and unloaded into a blower. This blower would blow the corn up in through the top of the silo. The silo was some 40 feet tall and about 30 feet in diameter. We had three of these silos to fill with corn. Corn would be cut in the field as much as possible on a regularly daily basis. However when we had to attend school, corn cutting was only done on weekends and on days off from school. We always manage to get the corn and on time.

I think that one thing that amazed me so much about this family was that they worked so well together. In spite of sibling rivalry and their individual quirks they all pitched in when work was to be done and got it done properly. George never wanted to get his hands dirty. He was the one that was always looking for the easiest job to do. Jennifer was one that pitched in and did whatever was required. She was more of a tomboy than a pretty girl. But Jennifer had a beautiful spirit and I learned to like her a great deal. She treated me like a brother, which really touched my heart.

I think the most difficult time I saw on this farm was in the winter. I had to attend school five days a week. But every single day I had to be in the barn before 4:30 AM. I never got back to the house in the evening before 8:30 PM sometimes 9:30 PM. If there were other things happening on the farm such as the cow having a calf, I was expected to be part of that.It didn't make too much difference how long it lasted into the evening. This left very little room for homework. But the teachers that I had in the school seem to be very well informed about me and were very understanding, and helpful. By the time the first school year was half over, I had pretty well made up my mind that I was going to quit school. I didn't seem to be doing very well in any one of my topics. I was barely getting C's. Besides I was sending as much money home to my father as I possibly could. The way I figure it if I work full-time on this farm I would be getting $100 a month. This would leave about $75 a month to send home to my dad. Some way or another some people around thare who knew me from school discovered my intent to quit school. They got together and took up a small collection to give to me. This impressed me so much that I decided to stay in school and continue my education. This proved to be a very intelligent move. My staying with this family and working for them last about two years.

I had been on this farm for a little bit over a year. I did have regular communications with my family by letter. The last letter that my mother wrote to me she told me that the family had moved back to the community and were living in Norfolk Connecticut. She pleaded with me to come back to the community. I wrote back to her and told her that I had no intention of ever coming back to the community. I told her that the abuse that I had suffered in the time that I was there was quite sufficient to last me for a lifetime. Her continued letters after that finally persuaded me that maybe the right thing to do for now was to go back to the community in Norfolk Connecticut. I finally quit working for this farm in the fall of my second year. My father came to pick me up and tuke me back to Connecticut. It was a joyous reunion with my family. But the oppressive burden of being in this cult sat in on me very quickly.

Chapter 25

Back With The Cult—For Now

By this time I was a junior in high school. Ben and John my two younger brothers were also in high school. The school bus came right to the front gate of the community to pick the children up for school. We attended a high school in Brkhamsted Connecticut. Ben and John were having a very difficult time in school. They were removed from the general track education and placed in special education class. This was a class for kids with learning disabilities. It did not take very long before Ben and John complained bitterly about the special track. I tryed to encourage them to keep on the way they were for now. A man from the community by the name of Jerry was in charge of the high school children. He is the one who had established the special track for Ben and John.Under normal circumstances it would be inconceivable to do things any different than Jerry had established. At the end of this first school year in early May, children in his high school were required to make out their schedules for the following year. Ben and John again came to me and asked me to help them get back into the general track. I saw no problem with doing this and thought it was a good idea. We went to see Mr. Dyer the vice principal. We walked into his office and sat down on the three chairs that were there. He looked up over his desk at us and called us by name and asked what we wanted. I informed him that we wanted to enroll Ben and John in the general track for the following year. He informed us that Jerry had already been to his office and set up Ben and John for another year in a special track. I looked at Mr. Dyer and asked him who it was that was going to school here. Was the state of Connecticut paying for Jerry to go to school here.Who was the state of Connecticut pay the tuition for. Wasn't the tuition being paid for Ben and John to go to school here. He said that it was for Ben and John but that he had to abide by what Jerrytold him. I told Mr. Dyer that if he did not enroll Ben and Johnin a general tracks for the following year that we would find another high school to attend. I also told him that Jerry did not have to know that this change had been made. But if Jerry ever came to him to ask him why the change had been made that he was to be told that I had threatened Mr. Dyer if he did not make the change. Mr. Dyer agreed to enroll Ben and Johnin the general track. He also promised emphatically that he would not say a word to Jerry or anyone else. He made us promise that this information would never leave his office.

During this summer at the community I was given the job of cleaning hot air registers from furnace ducts in people's houses. I enjoyed the job because it left me alone most of the time. The people that I cleaned the ducts for treated me politely. I was finding out what I already knew about people in the community. Most of the people were very nice and treated me with kindness. The management of the community were the ones that I had a problem with. I seem to have quite a bit of time in the evenings after work. I had always enjoyed doing things for people to surprise them. This worked extremely well for me especially when people had no idea who it was that was doing kind things for them. I was quite talented in woodworking. I made wooden gift boxes, jewelry boxes, or other boxes that people just want around to put things in that they valued. I would take these gift boxes and leave them on people's nightstands or on their dining room tables with small notes attached to them. Without my name attached people really didn't know where the gifts had come from. One nice thing about that was they could not return it. It was during this summer that I decided to make candleholders for all of the dining room tables in the main dining room. I wanted to do this without anyone discovering that I was making these candleholders.I wanted this to be a total secret that no one ever found out about. I worked on the candle holders for about six weeks. Each candleholder was designed to hold four candles. I made two candleholders for each one of their dining room tables. This project was quite involved. But I enjoy doing it nevertheless. I found that the best time to work on these candleholders was in the evenings when there was no one else around in the shop. The shop was never locked up and I had easy access to all of the equipment. On a couple of occasions I was very nearly coughed but it was only a nosy old man that wanted to see if anyone was in the shop. I was able to hide from him. As I was building these candleholders I found that they were going to be quite easy to hide. The hard part is going to be applying the lacquer finish. But I found that if I stayed up till two or three in the morning that I could get the job done. When I had these candleholders completely finished I snuck into the dining room at 2 AM and put two on each dining room table. I also found enough candles to put in each candleholder. No one ever caught me doing this and no one ever discovered who had made these candleholders.It would be 25 years later that I informed my mother who had made these beautiful candleholders that they had on their dining room tables. I described thecandleholders to her exactly as I had made them. So she knew that I was not lying. I also told her how many candleholders I had made and how I accomplish the job. She went back to the community and told the management of the community that I had done this. The next day the management gathered all of the candleholders together took them out in the parking lot and put them in a pile. They poured gasoline on them and set them on fire. Once again for the third time in my life my mother had betrayed me. But the candleholders had done the job for 25 years and had made an incredible statement. The statement that I got across to everyone in the community was that in spite of all the mistreatment that I hadsuffered that I did not hold or harbor bitterness against them for what they had done. I think that what really upset me was the simple fact that these people in this community had not acquired any greater understanding of Christian principles than they had two years before when I had been excommunicated. The way of life that was lived in these communities was nothing short of total domination by the leadership.

School started for next season in September. By the middle of November Jerry discovered that I had made the change and that Ben and John were in the general track. At this point all hell broke loose. It was again the worst thing that ever happened to humanity. A man by the name of Marvin was the top man in this community. I was called up to his office one day when I got home from school.

As I stepped off the bus someone was there to greet me and took me up to his office. When I asked him what the problem was I was informed that I had made a change in Ben and John scheduled at school without anyone's permission. I was also informed that Jerry was the one in charge of the high school children.He would make any changes that needed to be made. At that point I was asked to please repent for what I had done and to apologize to Jerry. I looked Marvin straight in the eye and asked him the same question I had asked Mr. Dyer. Who is it that is going to school? Is it Ben and John, or is it Jerry. In the special education class Ben and John were in a program were they were making absolutely no progress. It was time that a change had to be made. At which point I was asked why I didn't consult Jerry first. I said that approach had already been tried. My brothers were turned down and told that they needed to stay another year in a special Ed class. Jerry told me that another year in the special Ed class would havedone Ben and John a great deal of good. This was already the middle of November and one report card had already been issued. Ben and John were pulling C's and some low B's. So I said that the general track Ben and John were in was working and did them a great deal of good. I also informed them that this was not going to be changed. But I would use everything in my power to force to school and Mr. Dyer to keep the schedule the same without changing it back. This was not very much of an acceptable answer.

Well one thing I discovered for sure by coming back to the community. Things had not changed a bit. It was back to the old interrogation sessions that had been so unsuccessful for four years already. But what the heck these interrogation sessions that only failed for four years why not give them another shot and see if they might miraculously work. Every single day after school when the bus pulled up to the gate of the community there was somebody their to escort me to Marvin's office.Every day for the next two weeks from 3:45 PM until about eight o'clock at night the interrogations went full speed ahead. Sometimes with two or three men, sometimes with as many as six. These sessions involved asking me questions about my motives.Asking me questions about what I hope to accomplish. As well as informing me what a big piece of trash I was, and how evil I was, to have thought that I could take this responsibility on myself.To think that I could possibly get away with it. Most of the time I used the same tactic that I'd used before. While these men were interrogating me I was psychoanalyzing them. This defense mechanism worked for the first eight or nine days. It was on the 10th day of these interrogations that I noticed something was very seriously wrong.

At first whenit started I noticed that my eyesight seems to be narrowing. It seemed like I was developing tunnel vision. Within about a half hour to 45 minutes I had completely lost all ability to see anything. I had become totally blind. I could not even see daylight and I could not see my hand in front of my face. I was becoming extremely alarmed. I looked around theroom but could see no one. I could hear voices and knew who the voices were and where the voices were coming from but my eyes no longer functioned. I didn't know what was happening. The process from when I first noticed something wrong with my eyes until I finally made up my mind it was time to leave was about two hours. I finally got up out of my chair and walked straight forward. Marvin asked me where I was going. I said I'm going home he said you're going the wrong way. He turned me around. I left his office and felt my way along the wall and down the stairs to the apartment where my family was living. I went into my bedroom and lay down and fell into a very deep sleep. The Lord strategy actually was quite simple. This was his way of telling me that he did not want me in this community anymore. He had removed me the first time I was totally excommunicated and placed on a farm near Binghamton New York. He did not want me to come back to the community. Absolutely nothing wrong with what I had done to help out my brothers. The thing that I had done that violated God's will was to deceve myself into thinking that I could rejoin this cult.

The next morning was Saturday. At about 8:30 AM my mother came in to wake me up. She said that she got me some breakfast. I had not gotten undressed to go to bed the day before. I even had my shoes on. I got out of bed and got a laundry bag out of the closet and started to put my clothingeverything that I considered a value into it My mother asked me what I was doing. I told her that I was leaving. I explained to her that last night during one of the interrogation sessions that I had gone blind. But that now I could see again and I wanted to get the hell out of there before something more serious happened to me. She asked me where I was going to go. I told her that it did not make very much difference. I turned around and left. I walked out of the gate and down the road. I had been walking for almost an hour when my father finally found me. He took me to Winsded and got me a room in the local YMCA. He told me that they would make some effort to try to find me a job. He told me that he had paid for three weeks at the YMCA. I was to stay there until he came back and contacted me. Within two weeks he came back to me and told me that I could get a job on a farm in a local town. I was to get $25 a month and board and room. But the school bus would pick me up right in front of the house and I was going to go to school at the same school as before. This was a very good arrangement for me.

Chapter 26

The Last Farm

The farmer that I went to work for was a man by the name of Elton. He lived at his farm with his wife and two young children. The arrangement with this man was the same as two previous jobs Ihad on farms. My duties were basically the same. I was expected to be up at 4:30 AM to help with the chores around the barn and milking before I went to school. When I came home from school at 3:30 PM I was expected to get ready to start milking. My duties at this farm usually didn't end until 8:30 PM or nine sometimes 9:30 PM. Elton was amen who like to play the tough guy. When he gave an order he liked to sound hard and tough. I had no problem doing what I was told and most of the time we got along fine. After working on the farm for a couple of months I knew that I had a very distinct advantage over Elton in a lot of ways. For one thing he had to be extremely careful how we moved and the physical labor that he did. This man had slipped discs in his lower back.They were giving him a lot of pain. He also did not move very fast and he was not very agile. So it was going to be very easy for me to stay out of his way. I worked for this man for about a year and a half. We had run-ins with each other from time to time but it was never anything very serious.

On one occasion just before I quit working for him we had a major confrontation. When I went to school that morning I told Elton that I would not be home from school untill about 4:30 PM or 4:45 PM and informed him that he would have to start doing the milking at 3:30 PM without me. As soon as I got home I would be down to help him finish. By the time I got home from school it was almost 5 PM and the milking had not yet been started. When Elton came into the barn it was after six o'clock. We are feeding the cows with chopped corn. All the while he was cursing my family, myself, the community, the school and about anybody else that I was connected with. I listen to this stream of cursing for about an hour. I finally had heard as much as I needed to hear. Elton was by the silo failing a wagon with chopped corn. When he stood up and faced me, I grabbed the pitchfork and stuck it in his throat. I held him pinned to the silo for about 10 minutes. With pressure against his throat with the steel pitchfork. I proceeded to explain to him that I did not want to hear anymore verbal insults against my family, myself, the school, or for that matter anybody else. I told him that I had informed him that morning that I would not be home until almost 5:00 PM. I told him that he would have to be there at 3:30 PM to start the chores. I also told him that I understood that I had responsibilities on this farm but this is your farm not mine. This was early April of my senior year in high school. Graduation wasn't going to happen until June 15. I knew I needed a place to stay for at least 2 ½ months. I also knew that I didn't have the money to afford to rent my own apartment. But I told him that I was going to quit working for him in two weeks. For the rest of those two weeks we got along fine.

The state of Connecticut came to all the schools in our area in the last two weeks in March. They were testing the mechanical aptitude of seniors who would be graduating that year. When the results from the mechanical aptitude tests came back I scored in the top 10 students of the state of Connecticut. The second week of April of that year I was offered a job with a company in Torrington Connecticut. This company made spring winders and coilers. The job would be for second shift from 4:30 PM until 2:30 AM. I immediately went to see my favorite vice principal Mr. Dyer. I informed him of the job offer. I also informed him that I desperately needed this job. But I had no other way to support myself and had no income. He said that I should come in the next day and he would let me know what their decision was. The next day I went to Mr. Dyer's office. I was told that they had discussed the matter. They did not like the idea of me going to work 10 hours second shift and still make it to school on time the next morning. But because of my personal problems and difficult situation that the school would allowed it. I was also told that my grades would have to be kept up in order to graduate. I already knew that I had at least three very sympathetic teachers. I went to talk to them immediately. I told them what was going on and that I needed their help. They were all three very willing to assist me in any way they could. This is all that I could ask for. Again the Lord had shown me tremendous favor.

I had another run-in with Mr. Dyer. For my senior year I had signed up to take algebra one. I had great difficulty with general math in lower grades as well as in high school. Mr. Dyer did not discover that I had signed up for algebra one until after the first marking period of my senior year.When he discovered what I had done he called me into his office. He asked me how I got away with signing up for algebra one. I told him that I wasn't sure how it happened. I also informed him that I was getting a 98 average in algebra one. I told them that I found algebra to be quite easy and that I enjoyed the class. Mr. Dyer was very gracious to me. He informed me that because I was doing so well in algebra that school was going to leave it the way it was. He only instructed me not to go out for any extracurricular activities. This algebra class was also going to prepare me for working at a company a little later on.

Chapter 27

I Start Making It On My Own

I started the job at the beginning of the third week of April. The company that I went to work for was a company called Torrington Manufacturing. This was quite a large shop and had about 50 employees on second shift. There were five of us on second shift that were a part of an apprenticeship program. We were to get $2.90 an hour. We were also eligible for any overtime that the company required us to work. As a part of the apprenticeship program we would be given our toolboxes and the basic tools that we needed to get started. Twice a week we would be required for two hours each night to attend school. This school was to be conducted at the shop in the cafeteria. The school consisted entirely of advanced math. I had never passed a general math class in my life. And my senior year in high school I had taken algebra one. I loved algebra and at the end of the year I had a 98 average for the year. The math that we are to be taught was college level geometry, college-level algebra, trigonometry, and calculus. I had never had geometry or any of the other advancedmaths. But a few weeks into the program I discovered that it was not much different than algebra one. And I connected with this advanced math very well and very quickly. By the time the program was over six months later I had achieved a 95 average in all of them.

The work that I did for this company required basic skills and being able to read blueprints accurately. And to be able to do layouts correctly and within a few thousandths of an inch. These are skills that I had acquired in my years at the community making furniture. I was very adept at this job. Each job that was given to us to do came with a timesheet. Each operation was time intensive. I discovered that I could do all the nine hours work that I needed to do for the night in the first two hours. This left me plenty of time to go around and make friends with the rest of the operators at the shop. I got along very well with all of them. The other job I had was to grind grooves in the feed rolls for these machines that were manufacturing. The feed rolls that I was grinding grooves in feed the wire into the coiling point. The wire was fed into the machine against a coiling point at a continuous speed. A spring would form underneath the coiling point. When the spring was the right length a knife would cut the wire off. This was a fascinating job. After having been through the difficulties that I had endured in my life this job was simple. It was the easiest way I had ever had to make a living.

When I first started working for the Torrington manufacturing company, I lived at the YMCA in Winsted Connecticut. Within two weeks of starting his job I found a room to rent in Winchester Connecticut. Winchester Connecticut was only 7 miles from where I work. Getting back and forth was easy. My rent was also not very expensive. I graduated high school in June of that year with the rest of my class. I worked for this Company for about two years. But I soon discovered that working second shift was like having a part-time job. I got home at 2:45 AM and got cleaned up and went to bed. By 8:30 AM or 9 AM I was up. Then I didn't have much to do for the rest of the day until 4:30 PM when I had to be at work. So I started looking around for a part-time job. I soon got myself another job working from 10 AM until 2 PM for a small delivery company in Torrington. This kept me busy for the entire day. I liked the arrangement because it kept me out of trouble. This schedule left Saturdays and Sundays open to do more or less what I wanted. I didn't have to be back at work until Monday night at 4:30 PM. I also found other work to do on weekends. This arrangement lasted for about two years. But it was long enough to get me acclimated in society at large.

In 1968 I went to work for a manwho was manufacturing cribbage boards. We worked about 10 hours a day and I made fairly good money. He had another man working for him by the name of Bob. Bob and I work fairly closely together by talking with me and watching me Bob realized that I had some extensive personal problems. He told me that he wanted to introduce me to a friend of his in Massachusetts. At first I was very reluctant I didn't know if I wanted to share my personal problems with anyone else. After a few weeks of his continually asking me I finally gave in and said that I would go with him on the next weekend. It was a wonderful early June day. On Saturday morning at about 7 AM we left Connecticut and drove up to Massachusetts. We arrived at these peoples home just after 8:30 AM. Bob had already made contact with them and told them that we were coming. All the way up there he explained to me that the woman I was being introduced to had endured very similar experiences as I did. And that he thought that she might be able to help.

Chapter 28

Counseling With Love

The man of this home was named Jack. Jack had his own home remodeling business. Ruthann, his wife worked for the University of Massachusetts and Agawam. She was a personal secretary of the president of the University. They had two daughters, the oldest was Anna Beth. The youngest was Rebecca. They all for seemed to be wonderful people. We were cordially invited into the home. We sat in the living room for about 10 or 15 minutes just doing small talk. Then Ruthann started asking me personal questions. I started to tell her where I come from and some of the things that I had endured. After about an hour of talking to her and her husband Jack they made me an offer. They told me that from time to time they had helped other people with personal problems similar to mine. But Ruthann told me that my problems were by far the most severe that she had ever encountered. And she said by talking to me for a little while and watching me she could see that they were deep-rooted. Jack and Ruthann both agreed that they would invite me to live with them in their home. I could also go to work for Jack and his business doing remodeling. Both Rebeccaand Anna Beth agreed with their mom and invited me to stay in their home with them. Ruthann explained to me that she had had similar experiences when she was just a young girl. Her parents had been Christian Scientists. And through denying her medical treatment in an emergency it had very nearly cost her life. I was absolutely stunned.

I cannot believe that someone who didn't know me would invite me to live with them in their home. I told them that I needed time to think about this. They gave me their phone number and asked me to contact them when I had made a decision. Ruthann told me as we left that she was absolutely sure that she could help me. She said that she had done the same type of work with other people before very successfully. Her last words to me when I left were please calling me.

On the way home Bob gave me a little bit of history about this couple. We also talked about my personal situation. And I also was well aware that I could not continue as I was. I was almost totally dysfunctional in society at large. I knew that I had endured a total nervous breakdown when I was about nine years old. I was now approaching 20. I had not improved very much at all. My problems also kept me from any association with other people. I knew that I needed to do something to find some kind of a cure. There were two real problems in my life. The first and probably the most important was the hate and bitterness that I had acquired for the management of the community. I dreamed of how I would kill these people if I ever caught them alone in a dark alley. I had learned how to hate specifically, with purpose, and with conviction. The second problem was I was filled with so much pain that it was an all-consuming issue in my life. And there never seem to be an end to the pain. The nervous breakdown that I had when I was nine was a small matter compared to these other two problems. But I knew that I needed help before I got into some real trouble that would destroy my life. And here again the Lord was showing me favor. That next weekend I called Ruthann and told her that I would be up that day. She said that they needed little time to get the room ready. That I should come up the following weekend.

The next Saturday I showed up in Massachusetts at the Ruthann's home at about 10:00 AM. Ruthann showed me were my room was and where to put my personal belongings. Then we sat down and laid out some ground rules. I was to go to work for her husband Jack on Monday morning. But the pay would be based on the fact that I was living in their home. I was also expected to help with expenses around the house. I was given chores and responsibilities. It seems to me like a very good arrangement. She also informed me that she would like to start talking to me that evening. That first evening we talked from about 8:30 PM to about 2 AM. A lot of the things that we discussed left Ruthann in tears. We talked on weekends a lot of times till 2 AM or 4 AM. During the week two and sometimes four nights a week 2 to 4 hours a night. I am absolutely sure that this family had not anticipated the kind of emotional pain that they saw in me on a regular basis. These sessions lasted continually and a regular basis for almost a year.

During that entire year I worked for Jack and his business. During the day Jack was just as important in my healing as Ruthann was in the talking we did in the evening. After a few months the healing in me started to become quite obvious. I learned to squeeze out a lot of the hate and replace it with a few degrees of love. The pain in me was also controlled to the degree that I became functional in society. In all my life I think this was by far the most wonderful encounter and experience that I've ever had with other people in a close family setting. The other thing that Jack taught me was how to do remodeling. This would come in very handy and very useful a little while later. I had worked for these people for almost a year. When Jack and I came home on a Friday evening we had dinner as usual. After dinner Ruthann and Jack along with her two daughters Rebekah and Anna Beth set down in the living room. She informed me that they thought I should go on my own. She also said that she thought that we had made tremendous progress. The healing in me was quite obvious. I had progressed nicely and that I was almost a different person. The next morning as I was getting ready to leave there was one last thing that I had to do. I still had in my personal belongings that little statuette of the mountain sheep lying down. The one that was carved out a pure white stone. Ruthann had many knickknacks on shelves all over her home. I took out the little statuette and gave it to her. She was almost struck speechless. She knew that she was holding in her hand something that was precious to me. But something that was also extremely valuable. She didn't want to take it. I told her that I no longer had any need for it and that it was meant to be given to her. Besides I didn't want her to send me a bill for the work she had done on my behalf. She laughed and assured me that there would be no bill. I told her that I had been carrying around that mountain sheep for 14 years. Besides what that family had given me for free money could not buy anywhere else in the world. She was dumbfounded and asked me several times if I was sure that I wanted to do this. It would be 25 years later when I saw these people again that Ruthann informed me that the statuette of the mountain sheep was extremely valuable. It had been carved out of a gemstone and it was dynasties old from China. A gift like that could not possibly have been given to anyone else but to Ruthann. My entire stay with these people and I working with Jack in his business was done on their part with devotion and careing as well as kindness and love. I was treated as a son and a brother.

Chapter 29

Healing—On My Own

After this I came back to Connecticut. I got a job at Hitchcock chair again making furniture. I totally enjoyed working in furniture and working with wood it was the passion of my life. My father and mother and brothers and sisters had once again been excommunicated from the community. They were living about 4 or 5 miles away from the community and Norfolk Connecticut. My father was also working for Hitchcock chair. I worked for Hitchcock chair for about a year. I came home to the house one day and told my dad that I was going to Canada. I wanted to touch base with a lot of old relatives that I hadn't seen and many years. I took the next year to visit relatives in Canada and North Dakota. I stayed and worked in North Dakota for about eight months. I was visiting back up in Canada at the end of this eight months staying with the sister of my mothers. I came home on a Sunday afternoon and lay down for a nap. When I woke up I was trembling all over. I had perspired so heavily that the bed and blankets under me were wet. When I came downstairs my aunt saw the shape I was in and asked me if I was sick. I said that I didn't think so and she tried to find out more about what was wrong with me. I told her that I thought I had to go back to Connecticut in a hurry. I said that I didn't think that things were right at home. I told my aunt that something was wrong with my brother Nathan and my sister Luisa. I left in a hurry I came back to North Dakota. From there I called my mom. She told me that there wasn't anything wrong but everything was okay. I left that same afternoon and made it back to Connecticut in less than three days. When I arrived back at my parents home in Connecticut I discovered that my little sister had had appendicitis and that they had almost lost her. I also discovered that my brother Nathan had had acute appendicitis at the same time that I sensed something wrong when I was in Canada. Nixon's appendix had ruptured before they can operate. After an extended stay in the hospital Nathan recovered fine. I was once again being shown favor by the Lord.When I got back to Connecticut I went back to work for Hitchcock chair for a while. I only worked there for about six or eight months. While I was working there my father had a request from somebody that he knew, if we would come and do his friends roof. My father needed the extra money so he told them that he would do it. That same day by the time he got home he realized that he was unable to do the job. He took me down to look at the house. He told me to go to lumberyard and buy a ladder and get up on the roof and take a look. I went and bought a 48-foot extension ladder. My dad taught me how to measure the roof and how to figure out how much material it would take. He also taught me how to figure the price of the roof. My dad told me that once I give a price to somebody for a job that I should hold to that price. He also taught me that if my bid was too low that was my problem. He told me that it was unethical go back afterwards to the customer to try to get more money. I had to agree with him.I gave the people price on the roof and they agreed to pay that much. I had my first job as a home remodeling contractor. My father at the time owned a 1954 Ford pickup truck. We used this pickup truck to bring the shingles to the job and to clean up the trash and take it to the landfill. But if I was going to be a contractor I needed a truck. A year before I went to Canada I had bought in 1964 Buicks Skylark convertible. But during the previous winter it had gotten pretty banged up. I had about $1200 in the car. I had received back from insurance companies of people that had hit my car about $2500. So I was already making money on the car. I went to a car dealership that my father had done business with previously. When he asked me what I wanted, I told him I need ½ ton pickup truck used. He said you're just inlock we took one in two days ago. It was a 1965 Chevy half ton. This is just what I needed. The man wanted $1400 for the truck and asked me what I had to trade in. As embarrassed as I was I told him what I was driving. He said he wanted to take a look at it. I told him it was pretty well banged up. He took a look at my car and offered me $800 on trade. He went to his desk and wrote up the paperwork. He asked me when I could pay the balance. I told him that we had one roof that we ar working on now and had two others that were waiting. When he finish making out the paperwork he gave me the title and told me to go down to the motor vehicle and get the vehicle registered. When I had it registered to bring the title back to him and he would hold it for 60 days till I paid for the truck. This was a plan that I could live with easily. The man extended trust to me because he knew my dad. But it opened up away for people to start trusting me. I managed to pay for the truck in less than 30 days.

It was about at this time that I stopped by my dad's home on a saturday afternoonjust to talk to him for while. My dad seems to be down and that was not very normal for my father. After being with him for about an hour and a half I told him I had to go do some errands. He asked me where I was going. I told him that I was going to do some errands but that I also had to find an apartment in Torrington. He told me that he wanted me to find an apartment big enough for two people.That he was thinking of leaving my mother. My mother and father were living a very divided life. My mother was living outside the community with my father and family but she was going back to the community every single day with my older sisters to participate in that way of life. This brought great distress to my father. A few weeks after this I had a chance to talk to my mother. I told her that if she is going to make the Group of Brothers her way of life that she should take my older sisters and move over to the Group of Brothers and leave dad here for us to take care of. I told her that this divided life was killing my dad. And I informed her that if this continued for very much longer that we're going to be going to his funeral. I told her that this could not go on for very much longer. This must have really resonated with her. In less than a month she had talked to the management of the community and made arrangements for the rest of my family to move back to the community with my father in tow. I stayed in home remodeling and found that I could stay busy most of the time. When things got slow I could always get a job in the shop.

I worked at my job mostly alone. But when I needed help was fairly easy to find. And I learned as I went along. But I always tried to give people more than what they actually paid for. I always liked walking away from a job knowing that I given them more than what they paid for and that I did not owe them anything. I also try to do a good quality job something that would last in their home for many years. Also something that would add value to their home. I found out that by working in these ethics I never was short of jobs. And my name starts to get around by word of mouth, which was the best advertisement I could get.

Chapter 30

My Family And The Healing Hand Of God

From 1971 I did business with a small lumberyard in Winstead Connecticut. By the end of 1972 I started dating a young lady that worked at that lumberyard as a secretary. We got along very well. We decided we would get married. February 23, 1973 we got married. The wedding was a big affair mostly paid for by her grandparents. Our honeymoon was spent on a trip to Florida. I had never been to Florida, neither had she? The trip to Florida was a wonderful experience it got us started and got us to know each other better. When we got home we lived in an apartment that I had already rented. I also got a job with a larger building contractor. It seemed like a good idea and my wife Sarah was somewhat concerned about having a steady income. I worked for this larger contract for a little over a year. It was a very good experience and it also got me more knowledgeable in the building industry. I still kept my own business and work at it part time. Mostly on weekends and days off. I knew that I could make a few hundred dollars a week extra income working this way. Life went along about as normal as could be. We had our ups and downs, but we got along quite well.

Towards the middle of 1974 I went back to work for Hitchcock chair. I love making furniture; I just didn't enjoy working inside a factory. But this was going to have to do for now. The economy had slowed down somewhat to oil-producing nations of the Middle East had put an oil embargo against the United States. And it seemed like the best thing to do to bring stability to my home. And I still work money-remodeling business part-time. This arrangement would last until 1978. In 1976 my son Jeremy was born.

The birth was supposed to happen at Thanksgiving that year. Labor was finally induced on December 15. I was so very disappointed that the doctor couldn't wait two more days so that Jeremy would be born on my birthday. When the delivery happened I was in the delivery room. The doctor delivered the baby and gave him to the nurse who claimed his mouth and nose out. The nurse then turned around with the baby and gave the baby to me. I was so overjoyed at the birth of my son he is absolutely the joy of my life at that time. I looked at this tiny life that I held in my arms. He was a perfect creation, and a wonderful gift from God, and an answer to prayer. I had always wanted a son and a daughter. I held him up to the Lord, and dedicated him to God. I gave him his name Jeremy David. And then I turned around and put him in his mother's arms. I had come from a family of 14 kids. At any one time there were 5 to 8 kids in the house at the same time. So I thought I knew something about raising kids. Jeremy was going to be a challenge. But at the same time Jeremy was a joy.

When I was working for Hitchcock chair I got into the habit of getting up at five o'clock every morning. It seems like this time of day was a good time to be up. And I'm sure it was a habit from working on a farm and getting up at 4:30 AM every morning. It gave me some time to be alone with the Lord. It also gave me little bit of time to do some bookwork. And I did not have to be at work until 7 AM. After a few months of keeping this schedule I discovered that Jeremy was waking up at 5 AM every morning. So I got him up and changed him. And he started having breakfast with me between five and 6: 30 every morning. This was also good time because it give me a chance to talk to my son. And I found out that after a few months of this schedule Jeremy was always wide-awake at five o'clock in the morning. We also got into the habit of keeping Jeremy up at night quite late. So we put him to bed he would sleep all night and wake up with me at five o'clock. He was also able to read the clock because if I wasn't up at 5 AM at 5:15 AM Jeremy would wake me up. This also started to build a bond between Jeremy and me. I continue to work at Hitchcock chair until the spring of 1978. This was a perfect schedule; because it allowed me time to spend with Jeremy alone in the morning. It also got me home by 4:30 in the afternoon. I tryed to work my own business mostly on weekends. But the schedule is very flexible. This seem to be very good arrangement, and it worked very well for the first few years of Jeremy's life.

From the very beginning Jeremy was showing strong signs of being an independent individual. From the very beginning he insisted on doing things his own way. And when left alone for any length of time he always found something interesting to entertain himself with. By the time he was old enough to crawl around the floor, he was already getting into everything. If things got quiet in the house and Jeremy was not in the living room I knew that he was into something. I would very quietly walk around the house till I found him. Most of the time he was in the kitchen, either entertaining him with the storage cart where we kept canned goods. On quite a few occasions I found him playing by the bins were we stored potatoes and onions.For some reason this little boy like to eat onions raw. And the onions never seem to do them any harm. It also seemed from the very beginning that Jeremy was very bright. He caught on to new concepts and ideas very quickly.

By early spring of 1978 I was again working for myself doing remodeling. I had also started to make renovations in my own home. I took the oil burner furnace that we had in the house and disassembled it. I took the burner unit completely out of the sheet metal enclosure. I then put a wood stove into the sheet metal enclosure. This worked extremely well for heating a house. I always had a very good supply of firewood. Most of the time the firewood came from cutting down trees that people wanted removed from their yard.

In the summer of 1978 we got a small dog. This dog eventually grew to be about 20 pounds. This was a female that was black, white, and a beautiful golden tan. She had perfect markings. I want a small dog like her to keep an eye on Jeremy. That summer I was remodeling the kitchen. Just outside on the front lawn we had put in a small splash pool for Jeremy to play in. He was outside playing in the pool that had about 2 inches of water in it. And it sounded like he was having a very good time enjoying himself. Misty the dog was out there with him. After about an hour we heard the dog making considerable commotion. She was barking and sounded like she was very agitated. We looked outside and saw Jeremy trying to crawl down the hill towards the road. Misty was in front of him snapping at his face and barking. Sarah immediately wanted to run out and rescue Jeremy. But I restrained her and told her to watch the dog. Jeremy kept slapping the dog out of the way and would continue to crawl towards the hill. Misty got a hold of this T-shirt and tries to hold him back. This failed because the T-shirt ripped and pulled off Jeremy's body. Misty then got a hold of his diaper this also shredded and pulled off of his body. As a last resort Misty grab a hold of one of Jeremy's ankles just above the anklebones with her teeth. She braced her legs and held on and would not let Jeremy go any farther. Jeremy kicked up a considerable fuss because he could not get his own way and do what he wanted to. When I ran out to rescue Jeremy from Misty, I discovered that the only damage that she had done to Jeremy's leg was indentations in his skin from her teeth. She never broke the skin. And Misty had dug her legs about an inch and a half into the soft soil of the lown. Now I was convinced that this little dog would sacrifice her life if she had to, tosecure Jeremy, her charge. She was turning out to be the kind of watchdog that I really needed.Misty was a very intelligent animal. She also had an amazing distinctive personality. And I discovered that I had a real gift for working with dogs and training them. And Jeremy enjoyed the time we spent with his dog. Because it didn't take very long for me to lose this wonderful dog to my son. The dog was still mine technically but he was Jeremy's dog. I had taught the dog to protect Jeremy so well that when Jeremy needed to get a spanking I had to lock the dog in another room. If I ever gave Jeremy a spanking and did not lock the dog in another room, it was for sure that the dog was going to attack me and she did on a number of occasions.

I came home from work one day frustrated because it was one of those days when everything had gone wrong. Sarah had cooked a steak for dinner. And I was going to enjoy sitting down and having a stake and a can of beer. Misty kept hanging around the table, and I kept pushing her away with my foot. I did not want to share my steak with her. She was quite determined and didn't quit. I was down to four bite-size pieces of steak. And she was becoming highly agitated. I finally started paying attention to her, and told her that she was not getting any stake without doing something to earn it first. She set up and paid close attention to what it was I wanted her to do. I said you have to get up in your hind legs and walk around the kitchen. Which is exactly what Misty did she got up on her hind legs and she walked around the edge of the kitchen. She came over to my chair and sat down knowing she had performed her duties very well. I look at her and I said no you didn't do it right. I said over by the door you cut the corner off, and over by the stove you cut the corner off, by the refrigerator you didn't even go very close to it. You go back and you walk around the edge of the kitchen and don't cut any corners off. Jeremy by this time was laughing he was absolutely enjoying this scene that was unfolding. Misty very duty fully got up her hind legs and walked around the kitchen. This time however she rubbed her back along the perimeter of the wall, the cabinets, the door, the face of the stove, and the front of the refrigerator. She never allowed visible daylight between her body and the perimeter of the kitchen. And again she came over by my chair and sat down and looked up at me with her tongue hanging out as if to ask if she had possibly done the job right this time. Jeremy was laughing his heart out, Sarah also enjoyed this scene. Misty got the last four pieces of steak. Somehow I felt like I had been cheated. That night I fell head over heels in love with this little dog. She was going to be a joy to train.But it didn't seem like I had to do much training. She picked up what was required of her extremely fast. All we had to do was talk to her. If she misunderstood the first time by the second or third time telling her she picked it up very quickly and she was always extremely obedient. But this little dog had formed a bond with Jeremy that gave me the full confidence that she would always look after him. Every single night Jeremy gotMisty to followed him upstairs she slept on his bed by his feet. One night after Jeremy and Misty had gone to bed I was sitting and watching TV Sarah was asleep on the couch.There was no one else in the home. As I was watching TV I heard footsteps coming down the stairs. Halfway down the stairs the footsteps stopped. Then the footsteps started again and came all the way down to the living room floor. For a few minutes there was no sound. Then the footsteps started again and went halfway up. It was at that moment when I turned around.In the process of turning around I called Misty's name. Misty was not on the steps I stood up and stood there looking at the stairs. With me watching the steps for a few minutes, the sound of footsteps was heard again. The steps were heard going up the stairs and across the room by Jeremy bed and then stopped. I went upstairs to see if Misty was on the bed. Misty was on the bed sound asleep and so was Jeremy. This time when the favor of God was shown it came with a protector that stood by my son's bed and never left. This experience of hearing footsteps in the house especially around my son's bedroom happened at other times. I always remembered what I had heard and seen the first time.

It was in 1978 or 1979 that the Group of Brothers had moved my mother and father to their place in England. In 1980 in the summer about June we found out that my father had been extremely sick. three ofmy brothers, and myself made a long-distance phone call from my house in Goshen to England to talk to my dad. We got a three party conference call established. All of us got to talk to dad for about a half hour. My mother finally got on the phone from England and told us she could not allow us to talk to dad anymore that he needed to go and rest. About two weeks later we got word from the Group of Brothers that my dad had died. The four of us brothers immediately got together and decided to send one of us to England to be at the funeral. It would be a little bit difficult to come up with the money but we could manage. We called my mother to tell her that one of us would be coming to England to the funeral. She informed us that if anyone came to England to the funeral we would not be allowed to attend. We were told that we would be barred from the funeral.My father having died did not sink into me immediately. There was never any closure without a funeral and I could not go to his gravesite. About four years after the funeral I was coming home from work one day thinking about my dad. I had to pull over to the side of the road because of sobbing so badly that I could not see where I was driving. I sat by the side of the road for four hours and wept. It finally sank into me that my dad was no longer with us. I went home that night and sat down and wrote a 10-page letter to my mother and told her that they were no longer part of my family. I told her that my family had died with my dad. I explained to her about a lot of the pain and suffering I had to endure with this cultic community that was in large part due to her betraying me on so many different occasions. And I told her that I knew I was my father son because of my similarity to my dad in looks as well as disposition. The only contact that I had with my family since then is through my brother Solomon. And the only contact I have had with Solomon is because he has betrayed me to the community on three different occasions to try to have me killed. These people in this community have got to top the list of wonderful Christians in the world. I think I finally have gotten to the point where I actually understand this Christian community. Their origins is in the German youth movement after World War I. The man that originally started this community in Germany was originally all of that group of German youth. The mindset that operated in Germany at that time in the leadership was to rule by absolute power. This lust for absolute power drove the leadership of this community to physically eliminate anyone that they saw as opposition. This elimination of people that were opposed to them has been done in at least seven occasions that I know of by forced death. The

Jeremy was such an amazing joy. Every aspect of his life and his development and learning and growing brought so much joy to me. I never really saw myself as a father. Kids were always something that somebody else had and had to deal with. But Jeremy was never like that. I mean he was not somebody that I just had to deal with. Jeremy gave me his share of headaches. He was not always obedient and he had a slight spirit of rebellion in him when he was growing up. And I had to discipline him on a regular basis. He had all the same traits as any other child growing up. We just had to deal with each episode as it came along. That is just a part of raising children. But overall in his entire development Jeremy has been a joy.

In the summer of 1981 Sarah was pregnant with oursecond, child, my daughter. The people that I was working for the time had hired me to clear some trees off a piece of land. I needed the firewood for that next winter so I agreed to do it. On one of these afternoons Jeremy came along with. He was just 4 ½ years old. I had already cut the trees down and had cut the branches off. But I needed to cut these trees into fire place size wood. With Jeremy along I was sure that I could keep my eyes on him while I was working. The day started out beautifully, but got extremely hot in the afternoon. I guess I didn't keep his good and eye on Jeremy, as I should have. Every half hour to 45 minutes I would stop working to spend a little time with Jeremy. I also wanted to make sure that he was drinking enough water and spending time in the shadeBut something went wrong and by late afternoon Jeremy was feeling sick. So I stopped work and picked up my tools and headed home. I already had the pickup truck full of wood. That night Jeremy was feeling much worse. He didn't eat very much but he drank quite a bit of water. He also was running a slight fever. The next morning I went to work while Sarah took Jeremy to the babysitters. I came home early that afternoon and picked up Jeremy. I kept a close eye on him for the rest of the evening. But by eight o'clock that evening his fever was starting to go up. I took his temperature and it was 101. I got some cool compresses and put them on his body. About an hour later I took his body temperature again. His fever was now 102. I drew cold water in the bathtub and put Jeremy in it. The water out of our well was so cold that when you stood in it barefoot it would hurt your feet. When I placed Jeremy in about a foot of water he cringed but he never opened his eyes. I left him in the water for about 10 minutes. When I took him out and dried him off I again took his temperature.Thistime his temperature had gone up to 103. I was becoming considerably worried. I got ice out of the icebox and put it under his arms and on his chest. Again this caused him to cringe but again he never opened his eyes. It didn't dawn on me at the time but Jeremy was already in coma. After I kept ice on him for almost 45 minutes. After the ice had pretty well melted I again took his temperature. His body temperature now was 105.5. I knew that I couldn't make it to a medical center in time to save my son's life. I sat on the floor with my son on my lap with my hand on his chest. I cried out to the Lord for healing for my son. This was not Jeremy's fault.This was my fault, I had not supervised him improperly. I prayed for about five or six minutes. Suddenly I pulled my hand off his chest like it had been burned. I touched his chest again with the back of my hand. Jeremy was cold. I took his body temperature and it was 99. I took the thermometer and choke it down carefully to make sure that I took his temperature properly. I placed the thermometer under his arm And again took his temperature. This time his temperature was normal. Once again the Lord had shown us favor and his healing hands had been extended to touch Jeremy.

The next morning Jeremy was up at eight o'clock and came into our bedroom. He got on top of the bed and jumped up and down on top of me. He said "daddy you've got to get up. It's almost 8 o'clock you to be late for work". I pushed him off to bed and told them to leave me alone. He looked at with a puzzled look on his face. I told him that he had almost died on me last night. Jeremy crawled up on the edge of the bed and "said daddy I'm so sorry I didn't mean to almost die on you last night. I will try never to die again". My son and I had breakfast together that morning and came to a new understanding with each other. He promised that he would try never to die again. And I promised that I would do a better job of looking after him. and

September 22 1981, we were all at home in our house in the evening. We had already put Jeremy to bed. At 1030 at night Sarah's water broke. We had already made arrangements in advance for a girl that lived next door to us to come over and watch Jeremy. As Jeremy was already asleep all we had to do was to get this young lady over to our house to keep an eye on things. I went over to her house and got her. When she came over I took Sarah to the hospital. Her labor started at 11:00 PM. The nurse who was on duty on the maternity ward kept an eye on her. But by seven and eight o'clock the next morning the labor had almost disappeared. The nurses were ready to declare it a false labor. But when they got Sarah up to start walking around the labor started again. By 11 AM the nurse on duty after looking at Sarah said that she was going to leave. She didn't think that the baby would be born until five or six o'clock at night. About two o'clock in the afternoon our doctor came in and after examining her decided she was having a baby. The only people on the maternity floor was the doctor and a little old lady that was a nurse's aide and myself and Sarah. We moved Sarah into the delivery room. I had to show the little old lady nurse's aide how to set up a table. The doctor had gone into another room to gather up the supplies that he would need. While the doctor was gone I was stuck with doing the delivery. I let out a shriek and the delivery started. I had already delivered the head of the baby and the shoulders were starting to protrude when the doctor rushed in shouldered me out of the way and finished the job. I grabbed the blanket and he placed the baby in my hands. He cleaned out her nostrils and her mouth, and declared the baby a little girl. Once again I held this little tiny life form in my hands and praise God for a perfect little girl. I held her up in the air and dedicated her to the Lord and gave her name Melissa Anne. After the delivery the doctor was able to scare up some nurses to be on the maternity ward they had two patients to look after. I was tired and went home and went to bed.At 11 o'clock at night the phone rang. It was Sarah.She was panic stricken and crying on the phone. She said the doctors had discovered that Melissa was turning blue. That after a closer examination, and an x-ray of her heart, they diagnosed her as having a large hole in her heart. I tried to console Sarah. I told her that God did not give us this perfect little baby girl only to have a permanent problem or disability like this show up. The blood was going from the heart to the lungs and back to the heart to be pumped out to the body. But instead of being pumped out to the body the blood was leaking through the hole and going back to the lungs again. Our pediatrician came in the next morning and examines Melissa again. He came to the same conclusion that the other doctor had come to. He suggested that we send Melissa from Torrington Connecticut to Hartford to a specialist. Melissa was shipped off by 8 AM that morning. The next day at two o'clock in the afternoon we got a chance to talk to the doctor in Hartford. He told us that Melissa indeed had a large hole in her heart. But he said it was more like a separation in the muscle tissue. And he told us they wanted us to come to Hartford the next morning and we could hold our baby and feeder for the first time.

When we arrived at the hospital in Hartford Melissa was brought out to us. This was indeed our little Melissa. Even at two days old she already had her daddy'sattitude. After feeding Melissa and holding her for a couple of hours in our arms we went home. At this first meeting with the doctor, I asked the doctor if he kept records of everything that he found with my daughter Melissa. He said that of course he kept records. He was required to do so by law. Before we left the doctor told us to come in the next afternoon at 4:00 PM and we could take Melissa home. Weshowed up the next afternoon at 4:00 PM to pick Melissa up and take her home. The doctors told us that we should take an oxygen tank home with us in case of emergency. That if Melissa started turning blue we would put her on oxygen. They also wanted to see Melissa back to re-examine her after her pediatrician had seen her next. We gave him the date when Melissa would be visiting the pediatrician. And he scheduled the following day to see Melissa. At which time Melissa would be nine days old.

When we left the hospital and Hartford we did not take oxygen with us. We kept Melissa at home and on her eighth day we took her to see the pediatrician Dr. Gulliver. Dr. Gulliver took Melissa into a sound proof room to listen to her heart. After an hour and a half I went back and knocked on the door. Dr. Gulliver opens the door and handed Melissa to me. He said to take her back to the doctor in Hartford. Dr. Gulliver was very pale. I asked him what the problem was and he told me again take her to Dr.Comites. I tried hard to get information out of Dr. Gulliver but he would say nothing. But it was quite obvious that the man was somewhat shaken. The next morning at 10:00 AM we showed up in Hartford at the hospital. A nurse came in and took Melissa into a sound proof room to do an EKG tape on her. After she had run a 20-minute tape she brought Melissa back. She also gave us the stretch of EKG tape that she had made. Dr. Comites came in and look at the EKG tape he dropped it on the floor grad Melissa and went into a soundproof room and close the door. After two hours I started getting a little bit worried. At about two hours and 45 minutes I went over and knocked on the door. After knocking on the door for a few minutes the doctor finally opened it. I asked him if he was watching a football game or had he got distracted some other way. I said three hours and we haven't seen you. I asked what was going on. He told me that he wanted to examine the baby that we had there a few days before. What are you talking about this is the same baby you examine a few days ago. He said no the baby I examined a few days ago had a large hole in her heart. He said this baby has no hole in her heart. He said we must have gotten the baby mixed up with another baby at the Torrington hospital. I said this baby was never back at the Torrington Hospital. If she got mixed up it was here at this hospital. "What is it that you are trying to tell us I asked him". He said this baby does not have a hole in her heart. The other baby I examined a few days ago had a hold of her heart. I asked him if he remembered what I told him the first time I saw him. He said yes that he remembered that I had told him to be careful to keep records. He said we always keep records were required to by law. I told him to hang onto those records someday we are going to want a copy of them. I said "Dr. you have a gift for healing that God uses and heels many people through your hands. But this baby's healing was to be be done by the hand of God directly". I said "that's what you're witnessing. The hole in this baby's heart was completely healed in such a short time because God intervened". I said "this baby is Melissa Maendel, you can see that by the attitude that she has and she only nine days old". "This is my daughter she has got the same attitude her daddy has". At this point I asked Dr. Comites if indeed he had kept records of everything that happened to Melissa. He said that he had. I asked him if his records would indicate that the hole completely disappeared by itself without any medical intervention. He told me that he would be sure to put that in the records. And yet again we were seeing the favor of the Lord in our lives and yet again the healing hand of God was stretched out to us. And by this time I really started to wonder what is it about me that God is anfavoring so incredibly. By this time the Lord was starting to get my attention. Why is the favor of God poured out on me so extravagantly. Gods word says that he does not favor any one person above another. What is it about me that causes the presence of the Lord to be manifest in such a powerful manner. This also I would keep to ponder for another time.

This little girl Melissa Anne was going to be the second incredible joy of my life. She was already a major miracle and she was only nine days old. She had red highlights in her hair. Her brother Jeremy had dark red hair. Again it was amazing to see that this little bundle of life had very distinct and individual personalities. She was going to be totally different than her brother to rise. And the excitement had only just begun. With the first scare that she'd given us at her birth. Melissa was awesome to rise and again she was an extraordinary joy. She brought an additional spark of joy and light into our home. From the very beginning when Melissa was brought home, Jeremy wanted to be a part of her life. This would be the first time Jeremy had seen the baby. I mean really seeing his sister. He had seen her briefly in the previous eight days. But it never really had time to get to know her at all. Jeremy was a little bit upset that the attention that he had been getting for the past five years was being divided to include his sister. But at the same time he was excited to have a little sister. He really wanted somebody to play with. But he had a hard time understanding why he couldn't play with this two-week old little girl. He soon discovered that Melissa was going to have to grow up a little bit before she could come outside and play ball with him. We tried to make Jeremy as much a part of raising Melissa as possible.

As Melissa grew her true personality and character started to show. From the very beginning Melissa was filled with the natural love and joy of the Lord. Maybe this had a lot to do with the Lord touching Melissa's heart in such a special way. But Melissa even as a baby laughedeasily. And yet it seemed like the enemy was not done trying to destroy her.The next crisis in her life came when she was just about three years old. When I went to work that morning I knew that Melissa was not feeling very well. She seemed to be having unusual difficult time breathing. I chalked it up to being a cold. When I came home that afternoon earlier than usual because I was worried about my daughter. Melissa was still showing signs of breathing hard. And it appeared that these signs of breathing hard were getting worse. Melissa was sleeping in an upstairs bedroom. Sitting in the living room I could hear her wheezing and struggling to breathe.

At about eight o'clock that evening I had finally had enough. I woke her motherwho was sleeping on the couch and told her that I was taking Melissa at the hospital. I went upstairs and change my daughter and wrapped her in a blanket and got her into the truck. I drove her to the hospital and brought her into the emergency room. Within a half an hour the doctor in the emergency room had called Dr. Gulliverour pediatrician. Dr. Gulliver showed up, and it was obvious that he had gotten there in a hurry. He had on two different color socks. He very quickly diagnosed Melissa as having had asthmatic bronchitis that had turned to pneumonia. Melissa was in grave danger. For the second time and this little girl's life there was a very real danger of losing her. This crisis was far worse than the large hole in her heart. She was going to have to stay in the hospital for probably a week to 10 days. Within an hour and a half they had hooked Melissa up to four major IV's and the respirator.

They had tubes in her nose to help her breathe. The doctor informed me that if we had brought Melissa to the hospital a half-hour later than we did she would probably have died. I got on the phone and called Sarah and told her that the crisis that we had on our hands was a very real threat to the life of our daughter. At first she did not believe me. But she said that she was coming to the hospital anyway. When she got to the hospital and saw our daughter hooked up toall kinds of tubes she had a considerable change of heart. It was now about midnight. Sarah decided that she'd stay at the hospital with Melissa for the remainder of the night. The nurses provided her with a bed to lie down on and get some sleep. I went home and got some sleep because I had a job that I had to be on the next morning.The next morning when I got up I took Jeremy to the babysitter. After dropping Jeremy off I went back to the hospital. Melissa was already starting to show signs of improvement. She was starting to react well to the antibiotics. But I had also been praying most of the night for another healing touch for this little girl. I left and went to work. When I got to work I told the people I was working for why I was so late. I told him that my baby was in the hospital fighting for her life. They released me from work for as long as I needed to take care of my daughter. They told me to take as much time as I need. When I was ready to come back to work to finish the job. They asked me to please keep them informed of Melissa's progress. But they also would be praying for intervention from the Lord. I got back to the hospital at about two o'clock in the afternoon. Melissa was still in critical condition. But was showing signs of improvement.

I relieved her mother and told her to go home and get some rest. I stayed by Melissa's bed for the rest of the day. Melissa couldn't understand what was happening to her. But we found out that just by one of us being by her bedside and talking to her kept her quiet and she soon went to sleep. The doctors were also giving her mild sedative to keep her mostly in the sleeping state. She was being fed intravenously because by using this method it kept her asleep as much as possible. The doctors told us that by keeping her asleep most of the time was giving her body a chance to heal faster. I stayed by her bedside till about nine o'clock that night. When Sarah came in to relieve me I finally went home. This routine of one of us staying with Melissa went on for 10 days. After 10 days in the hospital we were allowed to take Melissa home. She was fully recovered. The four of us went out to dinner that night to celebrate. This was another major victory. But it was every single bit by the grace and mercy of the Lord and the healing hand of God had once again been extended to this little girl. We again saw without a doubt the healing hand of God and God's favor being shown us again.I decided from this point on that my work would take second place after my family and my allegiance to the Lord. I would never again put my work ahead of my family. From now on my family came second, my service to my God come first. Third on my agenda from now on would be my work if and when there was time. So far this three year-old little girl had been an amazing joy. She had also stretched the perimeter of our faith. It had also been made very clear to me that I needed to spend more time in the presence of the Lord. I could never have come this far without God's favor, or without his healing touch in my life. My children had both come through amazing crises. Both of my children were alive only because of the grace and mercy and healing hand of God Almighty. This was a major turning point in my life. From that time on whenever I saw my children I realized that they were not ordinary children by any stretch. Melissa especially was very important to the future plans of the Lord, not only for thepresent but also for a work that she still had to do in the future. It was very obvious to see in this little girl from day to day the presence of God was very much in her spirit.

Chapter 31

Raising Two Wonderful Children

For some reason Melissa favored her dad. I was the only one that she really tolerated to care for her. This put added strain on my already busy schedule. But it was also a tremendous joy to spend time with Melissa on a daily basis. But as time went on I look forward to the special time with her and her brother. And it also got to the point where Jeremy saw that I was spending so much time with his sister that he barged in and decided to make himself part of it. This also was a blessing because the three of us got to spend more time together. And while Jeremy decided now that his sister was over two years old he could start picking on her. I was able to control him most of the time. But the relationship of Jeremy to his sister was going to be a challenge and take time and attention to carefully allow this to develop. But Jeremy and Melissa both had the presence of God in and about them continually. After this incident neither one of my children ever suffered a serious illness. To this day neither one of them has ever broken a bone. They have been so well guarded and protected that it is absolutely amazing. Every time I pray for my son and daughter I thank God for his continual presence in their lives. And I think my daughter and my son both are beginning to see and sense God's presence. They also both know that they are not ordinary people. They both know that there's something different about each one of them.

Melissa's illness came in the fall of 1983. When we got her back home from the hospital my time of celebration continued for a long time. Our home life and family life got back to living one day at a time. But I started putting a lot more emphasis on being at home when I was not at work or in church. I was quite busy that summer with remodeling projects, and building add-a-levels. Add-a-levels in the 80s were a new concept. And I was quite talented at doing these projects. I was very busy for that entire winter. Our income was sufficient to cover all our needs. Jeremy and Melissa were both healthy and growing quickly. The other change that happens to us a few years before was that Misty was killed in 1980. She was very sorely missed in our family.

In the fall of 1983 our family went out to Massachusetts to Cape Cod. We rented a cabin out on Cape Cod not very far from the beach. We were going to stay there for about a week. It was well into the week about the fifth day when we went for a walk on the beach. While walking on the beach I noticed a dramatic change in myself. My vision went from seeing normal to having tunnel vision. When I came to I was sitting on a couch in the cabin. Sarah and the two children were standing in front of me trying to talk to me. I said that I was tired from the walk and just needed to rest for a few minutes. Jeremy told me "dad you have been home for about an hour and a half". I didn't believe him I said "we just walked in off the beach". He said "no that was an hour and a half ago". I knew at this point that there was something wrong with me. I also felt that it was a chemical imbalance in my body. I didn't feel sick any other way. I never had another occurrence of these attacks that year.In December a week before Christmas a salesman that I knew came to the house. This man sold insurance and I had used him on a number of occasions to acquire insurance policies for specific jobs. He said he was worried about me because he knew that I work for myself and he also knew that I did not have a disability income insurance plan. He said that if I ever got hurt on the job and was unable to work this insurance plan that he wanted to sell me would give me $1200 a month for up to three years. The price of this plan was $45 a month. I bought the insurance plan and it was to take effect in January of 1984. At the time I set this plan up I had completely forgotten about what had happened to me at Cape Cod. I set the plan up primarily to get this guy to leave our house because it was about 10 o'clock at night. And I also had to agree with him if something did happen to me and I did get hurt on the job I had never made any arrangement for another source of income.

From the middle of January 1984 the seizures that I had experienced at Cape Cod the year before, became more frequent.

The first one that happened I made an appointment to see a doctor in Torrington. He ran some blood tests that came back negative. By describing what had happened to me during one of the seizures he thought that it had something to do with my blood sugar level or my insulin level. He also discovered that my grandmother on my mother's side had been a diabetic. And he told me that diabetes goes from a grandmother to a grandson. I disagreed with him I did not think that I was a diabetic. What had happened to me was a chemical imbalance that was caused by something in my body. There was somewhat out of control.

In the first week in April I suffered the worst seizure so far. At this point the doctors in Thornton Hospital decided that they were going to send me to a hospital in Hartford for a CAT scan to check for a brain tumor. I was sent to St. Francis Hospital in Hartford. During the process of starting the CAT scan I had another severe episode. I discovered that when these episodes happened that large amounts of adrenaline was produced in my body to keep my organs alive. The severe episodes were causing my major organs to start shutting down. During the midst of this episode the doctors managed to draw a small sample of blood. They sent it to the lab for emergency analysis. The analysis showed that my blood sugar had dropped to 35. Normal blood sugar is 110. At blood sugar level of 38 a patient goes into a coma. During this episode that I was having I had an out of body experience. And I'm absolutely sure that I was in heaven. But I was told that I would have to go back that I couldn't stay. I came back into my body and started coming back to life. Two large orderlies were holding down my arms. I threw them off my arms like they were rag dolls. A young man 23 years old was sitting on my belly. He was a hospital administrator. When they saw that I was coming around they released me and stopped restraining me. The doctor told me that they had discovered my little blood sugar, and the rest of the blood test had just come back. It also showed that my insulin level was twice as high as it should have been.

I was taken back to Torrington Hospital. On the way back in the ambulance I went to sleep. It was about 3:30 PM. I stayed asleep for 24 hours. That next afternoon at five o'clock a doctor came to see me who was a specialist. He spent about 45 minutes or an hour talking to me. He told me that the information that he had received from me it was his opinion that I had tumors in my pancreas that were producing insulin spontaneously and sporadically. This condition that I had was extremely rare. In the preceding 11 years there had been nine other cases in New England. He also told me that he would talk to my doctor and do an evaluation to try to figure out what the next step was.My docter told me that they were going to run some tests to try to locate exactly where the tumors were. The test that Torrington Hospital conducted did not reveal anything. Four days later I was transferred to the Yukon med Center in Farmington Connecticut. This was a university hospital and was supposed to be up-to-date on the latest techniques and equipment. The day after I arrived at this hospital they conducted an angiogram. I was taken to the x-ray room and put on an x-ray table. The equipment was set up to take x-rays of my body. They had to cut an artery in my growing. They gave me local anesthetic, Novocain. After waiting 15 to 20 minutes for the Novocain to take effect they went to cutting the artery. But the Novocain for some reason hadn't worked. They gave me a second Novocain shot, this time it worked. I was layingstill and trying to mind my own business, at which point I heard the doctor say whoops. I looked up in time to see a red streak go down the wall. The doctor had cut the artery but did not have a very firm grip on it. This caused a spurt of blood to spray out. I asked him if this was a customary response when he was doing surgery. He and the nurse laughed and he told me to shut up. For an Angiogram a needle is inserted through the end of this artery in the groin up into the pancreas. There are four major arteries in the pancreas. The needle is connected to a pump. The pump injects dye under pressure while the x-ray machine takes 10 x-rays a second for 10 seconds. When the tumor is revealed it shows up as a blush on the x-ray film.

I was cautioned to lie extremely still and not to move. I was told that this process is painful but if I move it would have to be done over. The first series of x-rays were not a problem I had developed quite a high threshold to pain. The second one was worse, to third was worse yet. The third one I thought had worked quite well. But I also knew that I had surpassed my tolerable threshold for pain. The third series of x-rays left me sweating. There were two stainless steel bars one on each side of the x-ray table. These bars ran the full length of the x-ray table. I was hanging onto these two bars. They warned me that the fourth series of x-rays was about to start. I tighten my grip on the steel bars. I determined that no matter how bad the pain I was not going to move. I wanted an answer to the problem that I've been having. With the fourth series of x-rays came unbelievably, excruciating agony. The nurse came into the x-ray room jovial. We found that tumors we found the tumors was all she said. When she saw me she screamed for the doctor. The doctor came in took one look at me and had the nurse issue an emergency alert. I was lying on the x-ray table staring straight ahead gripping my teeth. My grip on the steel bars was like a vice. The pain from his last series of x-rays had sent me into shock. It took the doctor and the nurse 45 minutes to get me to let go of the stainless steel bars. They were finally able to pry my hands off the. It was another half hour beforeI wasable to get up. They also discovered that I had bent the two stainless steel bars on the x-ray table. I apologize profusely for the damage that I've done. This ordeal was a harrowing experience and one that I very nearly could not physically endure. But there was a victory in this because they discovered where the tumors were. They took me back to my room and I promptly went to sleep and slept for about 14 hours. I awakened the next morning just in time for breakfast.

The next morning the surgeon came in. He explained to me that they had found the tumors and that he was going to have to remove three quarters of my pancreas. But the part of the pancreas that he was able to save was the part that produces the insulin. But he also told me I would have to be on a fruit and vegetable diet because I would not be able to produce enough enzymes to digest any other food. He scheduled surgery for 14 April 1984. Sarah came in to see me that afternoon. I told her that they were going to operate the next day. I also told her that I wanted to see Melissa and Jeremy the next afternoon. She didn't think that she was going to bring them in. So I told her that unless she did I was going to refuse surgery. The next afternoon she did bring Melissa and Jeremy in to see me. Have to see Melissa and Jeremy I felt that I was ready to allow surgery to continue.

Surgery went very well. But I had to endure 7 ½ hours on the operating table. This left me physically extremely weak. The doctor did not think that I was going to survive. He came into the hospital next morning at 6:00 AM. He told me afterwards that the reason he came in so early was so that he could sign my death certificate. He said that he was very surprised that I was still alive. The nurses who were carrying for me said that I was continually unplugging myself and going for a walk.They couldn't keep me in bed. The doctor asked them how far my walks last. And they said about three steps. The doctor's instructions were to allow me to continue going for a walk. But when they picked me up to put me back in bed to double my morphine. They said that they were already giving me twice as much as I was supposed to get. He still ordered a slight increase. For the next six or seven days I was in intensive care. I found out afterwards that during the first four days after surgery they very nearly lost me.

After I came out of intensive care, I developed pneumonia in one lung.A respiratory therapist came in twice a day and help me clearly the pneumonia out of my lungs. This involved inhaling a saline solution for about five or six minutes. After which she banged on my back for about two or three minutes. Then she expected me to cough. I had 36 staples down the front of my belly. However in the world am I supposed to cough. She gave me a pillow she said here hold us over your belly but you have got to cough. After I coughed she showed me what had come out of my lungs.After that I never had a problem coughing. My recovery went extremely well. My stay in the hospital was 30 days. When I went home I was still very weak. My recovery lasted for almost a year, during which time I could not work. I was so thankful that the pushy salesman had almost forced me to buy a disability income insurance policy.I discovered very quickly that I could not eat anything but fruit and vegetable, a small amount of chicken or turkey. Almost everything else became a forbidden food. I discovered that when I ate food that passed through my digestive track without being digested was a little bit like to eating razor blades. The agony was excruciating and lasted for about three days. My healing as I said was almost a year. But my healing was complete. I just had to be extremely careful what I ate. By 1993 or 94 my condition had improved so that I could eat a greater variety of food. But the final healing occurred from December 2001,to December 2002. There will be more about these heelings in a later chapter. Although this healing happen through the hand of doctors and a long period of recuperation it was still quite obvious that during this episode the favor of God had once again been very prevalent in our families. And the healing hand of God was there in 1984.

The other thing that happened during this time of recovery was the benefit of the pushy insurance salesman was in our house the second week of December in 1983. This insurance policy start paying us $1200 a month and continued for a full year. This is one insurance policy that really paid off and I was for sure going to call the insurance salesman and thank him for making his policy available to us. It was also during this time of recovery that Melissa started to assist me and doing cooking for our meals. It was on a Saturday afternoon Melissa decided that she wanted pizza.It is okay get dressed and we will run to town and will get some pizza for dinner. No she said I do not want to get pizza I want to make some pizza. I have never made pizza in my life. I have made bread but in pizza dough is completely different. Well she "said I guess its time we started to learn". Well it can not get to bed if we get embarrassed by not making It right at least will be at home and we will have something to eat of it.

We got the ingredients and we started making the pizza though. But I made it the way I make bread dough. I let it rise and brought it out and kneed it down. I rolled it out on the counter in the size and shape of a square pan that I had. Melissa sat on the counter and helps me. We put tomato sauce on it. We put mozzarella cheese over it. We put onions, sausage, and green peppers on it.We didn't have any pepperoni so this would have to do for now. We put it in the oven at 265° and cooked it for the recommended length of time. I checked it every once in a while and I could see that it was rising more than I thought it should. I tried to punch it down with a fork around the edge as well as I could. When we finally took it out of the oven we had a large square loaf of bread about 3 inches thick. But there was no sign of the pizza ingredients that we had put on. Melissa took one look at this pizza that we had created and asked whether pizza stuffed was. I told her I believe it's in the bread. We waited and allowed it to cool for a while and then we sliced it and eat bread with pizza ingredients inside the crust. Melissa's reaction was "nice job dead". I knew that Melissa was going to be busy keeping an eye on my cooking. She was not real shy about pointing out mistakes that her old man had made. I was going to be disabled for at least a year. After being home for two or three months my strengths was starting to improve. It was at this time I was looking for some form of employment that would both take my time during the day and bring us a little bit more income. I found a job delivering newspapers on a motor route. The delivery process took about 2 ½ hours each morning. On Sunday it took probably 4 hours. But it paid $750 a month. And I could do this quite easily without straining myself and at the same time this job would build up my physical strength and endurance is little bit more.By the summer of 1985 I was fairly well recovered. I went to work for local contractor as a supervisor and to do layout on his projects. This lasted until the fall of 1987. It was at this point I went back to work for myself. I had reestablished myself with customers that I'd worked for before. I was able to pick up business quite easily. By the summer of 1988 the laws in Connecticut concerning independent contractors had changed. Contractors were now required to charge sales tax on their labor. I was no longer willing to abide by the stringent laws that governed only the money that contractors made. Laws no longer controlled or governed the quality of these independent contractors. So I decided to quit my job completely and go into a totally different line of employment.

Chapter 32

A Dramatic Change

In the summer of 1988 I needed to replace the roof on our home. We had already discussed the possibility of selling our home and moving to some other location. The replacement of the roof was critical to the sale of the home. I undertook this project by myself. It was not very difficult. But I made a serious mistake. In the process I was severely injured. I was taking the last bundle of shingles up on the roof. The latter slid on the bottom, and kicked out and collapsed I fell about 15 feet and landed flat on my back in the driveway. I was in excruciating pain. I lay on the ground for about a half hour. I was the only one home Sarah was down at her mother's house. I finally managed to move but could only crawl. I crawled into the basement and up the stairs. I sit on the couch for while but the pain would not subside. I got up and took a hot shower. The hot shower ease the pain in my back and my hips, but something was still wrong. I finally decided to go to the hospital. At the hospital I was x-rayed for a possible broken hip. The hip was not broken and they could not account for the severe pain in my back and legs. I finally went back home again after a couple of days took it easy. The pain to a degree subsided. After a few days I went back to finish the roof. It was while I was in the hospital and I started talking to a young man about owning my own semi-tractor trailer. But I didn't really know where to go to work or who to lease it to. He told me about a company in Bangor Maine that regularly hired own= operators. That fall after the roof was finished we put our house up for sale. In less than 60 days we sold our home and had the closing. After all the expenses were paid we had $50,000 in our bank account. I took $30,000 out and set up a business account for Dave's transportation. I went down to New Haven to a Kenworth dealership and put $25,000 down payment on a 1984 Kenworth conventional. The track only had 400,000 miles on it. This truck was equipped with a 400-cat motor, a 15-speed ranger, a single sleeper,locking twin-screw axles, and twin stacks. It was also a pretty Coppertone and color. I had already gotten my family situated in another home in Goshen Connecticut.

By this time Melissa was seven years old, Jeremy was 12. I was sure that if I own my own truck and leased it to another company that I could be home most weekends. I called the company in Bangor Maine and made arrangements to take my truck up and lease it on with their company on the following Monday. Sunday morning I left for the drive up to Bangor Maine. I came into the company's terminal on Monday morning and after taking an hour and a half driving test was hired on. I started hauling freight for this company, mostly paper towels and toilet paper out of OldtownMainepeppermill. The paper was being delivered to warehouses ineastern New York, Pennsylvania, Washington DC, and northern Maryland. Plus back halls were fairly easy to come by. And most of the freight that I hauled back went into Maine. It took me about a month or two to get well started and learn the roops and the shortest and most direct way to get to my delivery point. Once I got well started I discovered that I could make money very easily. And this was much easier than doing home remodeling. I also found out that I was home on almost every single weekend Saturday and Sunday. I always left Sunday afternoon to get to my next delivery point. And the other advantage was my freight routes most of the time took me through Connecticut and where my family was living was not very far out of the way. I could stop and see them during the week. I also stayed in close contact with them by telephone.My daughter Melissa went with me in the early part of 1989. We were in Bangor Maine and had the rest of the day off. We went to the mall to do a little bit of shopping. In the mall there was a pet store and Melissa saw a little Pomeranian puppy that she wanted to have. We decided to get this Pomeranian puppy female. This puppy became my daughter's joy possession. I helped Melissa to train this puppy that we had named Coco. Melissa spent a lot of time taking care of and training this little puppy. Full grown this puppy Wade 6 ½ pounds. She had a wonderful personality and wonderful characteristics. Her color was from dark red In her face to light red at the other end. Jeremy also became a part of training and caring for Cocoa. Although he wanted to act tough guy and didn't like to show his emotions very much it was quite obvious that Jeremy had fallen head over heels in love with this puppy.

For the next three years I worked hard for this company. I also drove myself almost to the point of exhaustion. I was able to turn more miles in a month than anyone else that worked for this company. And they also were a great help to me to show me how to stay legal. My pay was extremely good and the company was also making extremely good money on my equipment. Coco went with me quite often on these trips because I wanted her to become acclimated to riding in the truck. She soon took to riding in the truck quite well. And if I left on the weekend to go back to work and didn't take Coco, she became quite upset. My job with this company lasted about three years.While still working for this company I got a load of bailed shavings that were going to a feed mill in Pennsylvania south of Philadelphia just north of the Maryland line. I left Bangor Maine early in the afternoon and drove down into Connecticut. I stopped at a rest area to get five hours sleep. I got in at about eight o'clock that evening. I was going to drive down through Connecticut to New York City crossed the George Washington Bridge into New Jersey. I was going to get off the New Jersey Turnpike and cross over into Pennsylvania. At Trenton New Jersey there is a toll bridge across the Delaware River that crosses over into Pennsylvania on Route 95. As soon as I had gone into Pennsylvania I don't remember anything else until I got to the feed mill, which is about 110 miles from that point.

Chapter 33

The Lord Calls In A Marker

    The Lord spoke to me and said that he was calling me back to serve him. He told me that he needed me to take a message to the community that had so badly treated me as a young child. I told God that I couldn't do this because these people wanted me dead. And besides I had a son and a daughter to rise who were still too young to be left without their dad. The Lord reminded me that it was me that had made a covenant with him when I was in solitary confinement at 12 years old. And that he was going to have me honor the commitments of that covenant. The Lord also informed me that my children had always belonged to him. He told me that my children would always belong to him. That my children would never be lost and that he would care for them. He reminded me that my children had always been cared for by him.This conversation with the Lord lasted for almost an hour and a halfWhen I came back to myself my truck had started to cross a narrow bridge. This bridge crossed a deepriver gorge that dropped off about 75 feet. And if I kept going the way I was my trailer would never make it across the bridge. I had to back up almost half a mile to be able to get the truck over to the right far enough to make the left turn onto the bridge. When I completed the turn and cross the bridge I stopped on the other side by the feed mill. It was still only 3:30 AM or 4 AM so I went into the sleeper to catch a few hours sleep. At this point sleep was not an option. I had just come off a 1-½ hour stretch in the very presence of the living God. I also realized that I had attempted to negotiate with the Creator of heaven and earth. Since when did God need my advice when he set the foundations of the world? I knew house Job felt when God intensely questioned him. God already knew that I had two young children and that he had already touched their lives a number of times. He already knew that this community wanted me dead. He knew every difficulty and problem that I would ever encounter. His last message to me that morning was that he would call me when the time was ready to send you with a message to the community. I knew that the Lord had something planned for my future. It had been over 20 years since I've spoken with the Lord directly. But I also knew that there was nothing in hell or heaven that couldgets me to break my covenant with the living God. I was going to keep my word to the Lord even if it meant my death. I was at a point where I finally threw my hands up and I said Lord I know that I am yours and that I'm a profitof yours Lord Jesus and I will honor my commitment to you. I have no regrets in ever making his covenant with you. I don't know if I'm going to be able to pull this off but you do and I know that your presence will always be with. You have protected my life to this point and it is because of you that both my children are alive. I will answer your call. I delivered my load shavings and managed to get a backholl all the way up to Bangor Maine. There was a change in me after this encounter with the Lord. The presence of the Holy Spirit increased very noticeably. I also noticed an overwhelming presence of the Holy Spirit on every trip that I took. The Holy Spirit started teaching me the word of God. This teaching was to continue on a daily basis for 4 ½years

Chapter 34

A Thing About Dogs

Being an owner operator is something that I really enjoy doing. I really wanted to do this well into my retirement. And I thought I had found a way to make a living work to pay for my children's future. But problems in our marriage caused me to file for divorce in the fall of 1990. Our divorce was final in 1991. To this point Melissa had been a straight "A"student in all of her schoolwork. After our divorce was final she went down to a D. When I came home on that weekend and saw her report card I made a decision that I had to take her along with me for a week. I had a load of paper in large roles going to Minneapolis to a printing shop. The turn out and back would be a week. I took Melissa with me on this trip. Melissa was not yet quite 10 years old. As we rode down the road we spent a lot of time talking with each other. Cocoa also had accompanied us. This little dog was a sheer delight to have along. With her in the truck it seemed like there was never a dull moment. Melissa and I seem to connect on a new level. I think that she was afraid that because of the divorce her dad was going to leave. I assured her that I had never had any such intention. I promised her that I would always be there and I would never be very far away. We got to Minneapolis a few days later and got our load of paper off. From Minneapolis I got a load going right back to New Hampshire. When I got to Connecticut I dropped Melissa off at the house. It was Friday so I decided to stay home for the weekend.

It was on this weekend that we got a hold of a Dog Fancier magazine. We found an advertisement in this magazine from a place in Washington Missouri that raised Pomeranian puppies. I really wanted to breed Cocoa and raise some puppies. I called the woman in Washington Missouri and asked her if she had any male puppies. She said that she had one male left from a letter. But the dog was only seven weeks old and would need a few more weeks to be old enough to ship. She said with air freight to Bangor Maine the dog was going to cost $750. I agreed and sent her a certified check for that amount. When the dog was 12 weeks old she called me and told me that she was going to ship the dog the next day. That was a good arrangement because two days later I would be in Bangor Maine when the dog arrived.

Although Melissa and I had planned to get another dog I did not let her know that I had actually made the arrangements and purchased one. In fact I told her that I was not sure that this time we could do that. I told her that I thought it might be too much of a strain. She was very upset but I told her that we would talk about it again sometime in the future. I wanted to put her off as much as I could. This would give me time to actually acquire the dog and bring him home with me in the truck. When I got to Maine I took a few hours off in the afternoon and went to the airport. I already found out what flight to his dog would arrive on a new when the flight was coming in. I got to the airport about half an hour before the flight came in. I was waiting at the terminal desk in the cargo section of the airport. A man came in out of an airplane carrying a large cage. As he came closer I saw that the cage was completely filled with shredded newspaper. As he came in the door of the terminal I asked him "where in the world is my dog". All he did was grinning from ear to ear and point to the cage. I said "that's nothing but a cage full of newspaper". He said "you just keep talking that dog already recognizes your voice as the owner". He set the cage on the counter and the newspaper started jumping around. I opened the door of the cage and this pretty little Pomeranian puppy came to the edge of the cage and without breaking stride this puppy walked right off the edge of the counter as if to say you bought me you catch me. I caught the dog. This dog and I connected immediately. But this dog was going to have an attitude. He was a live wire.

On my way south through Connecticut I stopped to see Melissa. As I walked up to the house both my children were home. They greeted me at the door and saw that I had something in my coat pocket. They were eager to see what it was but I restrained them. I very carefully pulled Cody out of my pocket. That is what I had named this puppy. Melissa instantly fell in love with him and so did Jeremy and it was obvious from both of their expressions and behavior that this dog had made a big hit. But by the time I got to Connecticut I was not real sure that I like Cody very much. So I decided to leave him home on the first few trips. And instead took Coco along. This went along fine for a few weeks. One weekend when I stopped at the house on a Friday afternoon I walked into the house with Coco. Cody beat up on her for a few minutes and then it looked like he was kissing her and try to make up with her.But while I was sitting down Cody kept coming over and jumping up on me. I kept pushing him away from me with my foot. This happened three or four times. Finally I got frustrated and made like I was shooting him with my finger. As soon as I said bang this dog rolled over on his back with his tongue hanging out and acted like he was deader than four o'clock. I said Cody come on it wasn't even loaded. Cody didn't move after yelling at him a few times, Melissa being upstairs heard the commotion. She came running down the stairs and saw Cody laying on his back with his tongue hanging out. She yelled at me and accuses me of killing her dog. And I told her I'd only shot him with my finger and that they were not loaded. At this point I got up out of my chair and took a step towards Cody to kick him in the butt. Cody immediately jumped up and ran across the room and sat down with his tongue hanging out laughing at me. This was enough, Cody had my attention, he had a serious attitude problem that needed corrected but he had a very distinctive personality and a sense of humor that I have never seen in very many dogs in my life. I fell in love with him. For the next few weeks I took Cody along with me on my trips and started to train him. This dog was an absolute joy. But I soon discovered that I own Coco and that Melissa actually owned Cody. That did not take very long and I had just lost a valuable little puppy. Cody was also red. From the tip of his tail he was light red but farther up along his back the red color became darker until he developed into a striped between his shoulders and to the top of his head that turned almost black. He was a pretty puppy and the perfect match for Cocoa.

The first-time Coco had puppies she had the first one was stillborn the second one survived. We tried everything we could to revive the first puppy but never managed. When a second copy was finally delivered Coco was laying in a box that we had put her in nursing the puppy. We heard a scratch at the door. Cody wanted to see what was going on. He trotted in and stuck his nose over the edge of the box that Coco had the puppy in. Cocoa immediately grabbed hold of his nose with her teeth and Cody retreated backwards till he got to the door. At this point Coco let him go. We didn't see or hear anything from Cody for about 10 minutes and we were starting to feel a little bit sorry for him. After all he was the daddy. In a few minutes however we heard a scratch at the door. It was Cody he whined a few times. Cocoa stuck her nose over the edge of the box and watched him. Cody crawled across the floor on his belly till he got to the edge of the box. He dropped three pieces of dog food on the floor by the edge of the box and crawled backwards till he got to the door. He never took his eyes off of Coco. I guess he did not want to get his nose bit against. For the next week this is how Cody fead his mate. In fact we supplied Coco with water by the edge of the box but Cody had to bring the food. This was a site that we all enjoyed a great deal.

Over the next three or four years we raised 13 puppies from this pair. Most of the time when Coco was ready to deliver puppies I had to take her with me in the truck. They were great entertainment on the road. And everyone at all truck stopsloves to see the Pomeranian puppies. Melissa and Jeremy were also having a wonderful time raising and caring for the young puppies. Now that is something special to show to all thire friends. I never had too much trouble selling the Pomeranians. They seem to sell fairly well. But it was never a very moneymaking enterprise. But it was not being done to make money. Whenever I took Cody in the truck with me he seemed to pay close attention to me. After he had been with me a few times he could tell when I was becoming very tired. He also learned what the signs look like that indicated a rest area. And when he wanted to stop he would sit and look for a sign that indicated a rest area. When I got too tired to stand in the sleeper and put his front feet on the back of my seat and stick his cold nose in my right ear. If I didn't pay attention he would do it to the left ear. If I still didn't pay attention he would grab a hold of my ear lobe with his teeth. Finally I told him get over the passenger seat and wait for a rest area. We would always pulled into a rest area and hang out for an hour or two. One time I really wanted to see if he knew what the sign to the therest area was all about. So when we came to a rest area he saw the sign he kept looking at me but I didn't slow down I went right past the rest area. When he saw that I was not going to stop he immediately started barking. He jumped in the sleeper and stood on the back of my seat and grab my righty ear with his teeth but this time you serious. I said okay get over the passenger seat and will stop on the access ramp back onto the road. Cody never let me forget that I missed once.

I was running a flatbed trailer from time to time out of Main. On my way back through Connecticut on Friday evening I came down through Hartford and along Route 44. Driving along one section of Route 44 going west, the road bends slightly to the left. I guess I must have been paying attention to Cody. The right front wheel of my truck was slightly off the road. The front right tire hit some old wood guardrail posts, knocking them down. When I felt the contact with the guardrail posts I immediately pulled the truck to the left. As I did so I looked in the right rear view mirror. At the time I was hauling a load of lumber out of Maine. I was running about 85,000 pounds gross. When I looked in the right rear view mirror, I saw that the wheels on the right of the trailer had gone completely off the road. But the wheels as they went off the road did not make contact with the ground. They stayed up in the air. The shoulder of the road dipped slightly down and away from the blacktop at about 10° angle. The other thing that was strange was the airbag suspension on my trailer did not expand to force the axles on that side down. The trailer had been miraculously suspended in midair. There was no physical explanation why the wheels should stay in the air when the whole side of the trailer went off the road. The truck came back onto the highway and I kept on driving. I mentally mark the spot where this had happened. On Saturday afternoon Jeremy and I went back to the spot and examined the physical evidence on the ground. The guardrail posts that I'd knock down were very rotten and were in need of coming down anyway. But why would my trailer go off the road and stayed airborne. The front wheel of the tractor had made a tire mark in the soft dirt where it contacted the guardrail posts and where it went off the guardrail posts back onto the road. But the imprint in the soft dirt was not deep enough to account for the waight of the truck. We started looking around through the woods off the road in that area. About 75 feet into the woods at about 35° angle off the road, there was a creek that ran under the highway. The creek dropped about 50 feet below the edge of the road. Around the large culvert that ran under the road there were two massive concrete walls that guided this creek into the culvert. If my truck had continued on the course it started when it went off the road the truck would have gone down into the cul-de-sac and I would have been killed. All of the lumber on the trailer would have in ended up on top of me. Again the Lord was displaying clearly that he was always with me and was protecting me at every turn.

Chapter 35

Law Enforcement And Positive Evidence

Itwas in about 1992 or early 1993 when I got word through the grapevine of truck drivers that I knew that the Maine State police were looking for me to. I could not imagine what the Maine State police wanted with me. I started making some phone calls and was directed to the US Atty.'s office in Bangor Maine. I was informed that they would really like to speak with me. They wanted to know if I could make arrangements to come to Maine. I asked him to please give me a week or 10 days to work out a plan to come up to Bangor to talk with him. After about a week I ended up in Connecticut with a load of freight out of Ohio. I unloaded my freight on Friday. I called my dispatcher and told her that I needed a couple of days off. On Monday morning I drove the car that I borrowed up to Bangor Maine. I checked in with the US Atty.'s office and told him who I was. After waiting for about a half hour two gentlemen came out to see me. They took me into a room and started asking me questions about my trucking experience and other experiences I had in Maine. These two gentlemen were Maine State police officers who were in service to the US Atty.'s office.

They wanted information that I had about a plan with a half dozen truck drivers from Maine to haul marijuana out of Arizona. I gave them all the information that I had. I was even able to tell them where they would very probably find a large amount of cash that they had never yet discovered. 10 truck drivers had already lost their trucks and seven of them had already lost their homes and were spending up to 10 years in state prison. After they were finished questioning me they asked me if there was anything I wanted in return for helping them. I had apparently helped him a great deal. I asked them if they had access to the FBI computer in Washington DC.They said that they did. I asked him to please run and name for me through the FBI computer and see what information they could get. They want to know what the name was. I told them that the name was Jack Mason. I told them that he had been a member of the Group of Brothersfrom Reston New York. I told them that I thought originally Jack Mason had come out of Louisiana. But that he had been with this community for seven or eight years. They ran his name through the FBI computer and came back with an answer. They were able to verify this man as the same one that had lived with the Group of Brothers.They told me that they were able to track him but that his named all of a sudden ceased to exist. This had apparently happened without any death certificate or any other reported crime against him or any explanation for the reason of his disappearance. But the way it was listed in the computer it appeared that he had died or been killed suddenly. They told me that the chances of him having just gotten lost were very slim. They said from a police officers point of view they would say that he was probably murdered. This verified for me that he was another one of those people that Johnson or his son Silas had had killed. Jack Mason had been guilty of the major crime of disagreeing with von Kopf. He had also helped me out in a time of majorcrisis, which was also very disagreeable with von Kopf. The other thing that really amazed me about these people that were disappearing and very apparently about their demise was that other leaders and elders at the Group of Brothers must have seen and known that these killings were going on. However nobody ever said a word or did anything on the people's defense that were being singled out. And no one ever reported that anyone had come up missing and probably be killed. This was all handled as normal operations of a Christian community.

Every once in a while I was running a flatbed trailer. I hauled a load of lumber out of Bangor Maine that went down into Maryland. I deliver the load of lumber, and was sent down to Delaware to a pipe shop to pick up load of steel pipe going back to New Hampshire. I was down at the pipe shop by 11:00 AM, but for some reason the factory didn't even begin to load me till almost 4:00 PM When I finally got the pipe on my trailer and got my paperwork and was out of there it was after 5:00 PM. I was frustrated because it was Friday afternoon and I really wanted to see my children that weekend. I started north on Route 95. Traffic was somewhat heavy and going was going to be slow. By the time I got into New Jersey it was already close to 7:00 PM. I kept on pushing north I needed a faster way to get through New York City than going over the George Washington Bridge.I decided to go to Trenton and go north from Trenton New Jersey. Trenton New Jersey had just built a new Beltway around the eastern edge of the city to keep traffic out of the city itself. This new road was all concrete and was good to drive on. It would also be a lot faster because this new road was not very well used yet. I was running north with a dozen other trucks. At one spot this new road makes a real wide 90° turn from going west to turning back to going north. I hit the stretch of road doing almost 70 miles an hour. Before I realized what was happening I was driving on a section of road that had stone littered all over it. A dump truck had come around the corner and spilled out a large quantity of one and ½ inch stone all over the concrete road. I was in the process of maneuvering around the this corner to the right. As soon as I hit the stone my truck started sliding to the left. I was in the far right lane. The truck slid all the way across the road and the guardrail was not very far away. At this moment I cried out to the Lord. "Lord Jesus rolled out the red carpet because it looks like I'm coming home". I had no physical way to get the truck to stop sliding there was just too much stone spread out over this part of the road. As soon as I cried out to the Lord the truck instantly stopped sliding right at the edge of the pavement. The truck proceeded on top of the stone as if it was on dry concrete road and went around the corner very nicely. When I got straightened out the truck drivers in back of me were yelling at me wanting to know what kind of a magic act that pulled to get the truck to stop sliding. They told me that I was on top of all this loose stone and was rolling like I was on marbles. I told them I had nothing to do with it that what they witnessed was an act of God.Once again the Lord Jesus had shown me favor and displayed his continual presence with me that he promised so many years ago. I had come through this ordeal that could have very easily destroyed my truck and probably killed me without a scratch praise God.

Chapter 36

End Of An Era And The Lord Calls
Me To Service

By 1994 I had gotten into running a flatbed trailer full time. A lot of the loads that I hauled needed to be covered with tarps. But lifting and moving the tarps around got to be a lot of trouble. I was starting to have severe pain in the fifth vertebrae in my back. This had been giving me trouble for a few years. It seemed like the vertebrae would heal together and then when it was put under strain like lifting tarps it would pop apart. Bone chips were pinching the spinal column and I was being paralyzed from the waist down. But I was not going to endure back surgery. On many occasions I would lie in the bunk of the truck and put myself in traction as well as I could. If I could stay in this position for a couple of hours my back seemed to reposition itself so that the excruciating pain would go away. But because of the problems I was having with my back I knew that my truck driving days were numbered. It would not be very long before I was going to have to find another way to make a living. By 1996 I had pretty well decided that I'm going to have to get rid of my equipment. There were some of my father's relatives living in Alliance Ohio. I started running steel of the Ohio steel mills to New York City, New Jersey, and into Connecticut. And I was still getting home on most weekends. There is an Assemblies of God church in Alliance Ohio that my uncle and aunt we're going to. I started going to church with them on Sunday mornings whenever I was in Ohio. I also could sense that I was I was nearthe time when the Lord would call me to go is a witness for him back to the community. September 9, 1996 was a Sunday. I had parked my truck at my uncle's house. There were almost 150 people in this church on that Sunday morning. My uncle and aunt and I sat in the back pew and I were sitting in a position next to the aisle. When the service started we were standing in praise and worship and singing songs. The Lord spoke to me and said that he wanted me to go to the community as a messenger. This is a voice that I heard with my ears. And I was responding to the Lord by speaking verbally. I said "Lord okay I will go. But I have never done anything like this for the Lord before" I didn't quite know how to get started. How do I contact these people? I made up my mind that I was going to go up to the altar for prayer. I started down the aisle but about 10 feet the Lord stopped me. He said to me "the prayers that you want to pray will be answered when and where they need to be answered. Just go and do what I sent you to do". I went back to my place and stood in praise and worship for a few more minutes. I was still somewhat confused about how I was supposed to go about doing this. Also I was somewhat concerned because these people had made active moves against me to kill me. Again I started down the aisle for prayer. And as before the Lord knew my heart. He stopped me again, this time he said "take your hearing aids out you don't need them anymore. This is a gift I'm going to give you to show you that I can take care of you. Just go and do what I've sent you to do". By this time I was somewhat rattled. The entire congregation of the church was watching me. And they were listening to my side of the conversation. But they did not understand or hear the conversation from him the Lord. When I took my hearing aids out and put them in my pocket I realized there was a tremendous amount of noise in the church.

But I still did not connect to my hearing having been restored. By this time in my life I had been diagnosed as having lost 98% of my hearing. I was literally deff as a post. I could hear almost nothing. And I talked very loud because I could not hear my own voice. When the Lord said to take my hearing aids out, my hearing aids went dead. When the batteries in your hearing aids go dead they act like ere plugs. I went home after church and lay down in my truck for about an hour. I was still quite rattled. I went to my uncle's house to talk to him for a few minutes. He was playing with something in his hand. What he was playing with he threw. It landed about seven or 8 feet away from me on the carpet. I sat bolt upright. I have heard it hit the carpet. I asked him what he had just thrown. He said that he was a piece of paper. I asked him if he had heard it hit the rug.He said no it is just a piece of paper. I told him that it had made a distinct sound when it hit the rug. I was talking so loud that my cousin woke up and came out of her bedroom. She looked at me and said "Dave you're not even wearing your hearing aids." I said "yes but that piece of paper when it hit the rug it made a sound. I heard it make a very distinct sound". It was at this point when I first start to realize that the Lord that morning in church had restored my hearing. It was getting late and I had a load of steel on a trailer up in Warren Ohio that had to go to Chicago. I left and went up to the truck stop in Waren Ohio and hooked onto my trailer. I got fuel and went into the fuel desk to talk to the people.I bought a 60-minute phone card for $20. I called my daughter and told her my hearing had been totally restored. She was very excited and I had her crying on the phone. My daughter at this time was 14 years old. I had never heard her true voice before. I said Melissa you've got to do me a favor. She wanted to know what the favor was. I said you have to talk to me. I just want to hear your voice. I have never heard your true voice before. I said you are 14 years old, I raised you from being a baby, and I've never heard your true voice before. I said please just talk to me for an hour. She asked me what she was supposed to say. I said go upstairs in the back room and get the Encyclopedia Britannica M, and start reading in the middle and read to the end of the book. By then I will have heard your voice and I would remember what you sound like. She said dad you are crazy. I said you should be on my side I said you have heard my voice all your life. This is the first time I've ever heard your true voice and you have a beautiful voice. Please just talk to me for a while. We used up the 60 minute phone card talking to each other. For the first time in my daughter's life I could hear the beautiful tones she had in her voice. I realized that I needed to talk to my son. I asked Melissa where Jeremy was. She told me where he was at that time. She gave me the phone number where I could reach him. I bought another 60-minute phone card for $20 and went through the same process with my son. I told my son what had happened that morning in church, and that my hearing had been totally restored. He was very excited. These two children were getting tired of screaming at their father over the phone. I talked to my son for the entire 60 minutes on that phone card and like Melissa I discovered that I'd never heard his true voice before. This was definitely an awesome day for me personally but also for my two children. The Lord had once again favored our family and shown us grace and mercy and his healing hands were once again extended to our family.

I knew very well from the beginning that this contact with the people from Pine Hill, the Group of Brothers was going to be a problem. I knew very well from past experience that there was no way that I could trust them. They had tried so many times in the past to force me to commit suicide or to kill me. But I had a mission to complete for the Lord.There is no way while I was still alive that I would be disobedient to my heavenly father. I got a telephone number for Pine Hill and called them. When I asked to speak to somebody in charge there was immediately an attempt made to prevent me from talking to the people I wanted to. The only other thing I could do was to leave a message, which is what I did. I was called back within a few days. I told the people at Pine Hill that I needed to talk to them to try to come up with some kind of settlement for the abuse that I had suffered as a child.A meeting was set up at a restaurant in New Palts New York. I knew where this restaurant was. I had been there before since I had left Pine Hill. On the designated day a half hour before their arrival Jeremy and myself were at the restaurant. We were met there by Silas, and another man. They asked me what I wanted. And I had not yet received a message that the Lord wanted me to deliver to these people. I have been in situations like this before. And what I've always done is make some kind of communication with people until the messages given to me. There is always a purpose for this waiting before the message is delivered. So I told Silas that I wanted them to release my family and my other relatives that they were holding hostage in their community. That was not a topic for discussion. And I said well something needs to be done to bring some kind of settlement for the massive abuse that I suffered as a child in their care. I told him that I could not think of any other community, Christian or not that brutalized young people to the degree that we had been brutalized as children. I also informed them that there was no statute of limitations on this severe kind of child abuse or slavery. Silas told me that I should think about my children and about their welfare. I told Jeremy to keep the other man entertained for a few minutes. Silas had already gotten up from the table to leave. I followed him outside. I looked this man right in the eye and told him that if he had a problem with me to deal with me. My children were not a part of this and his threatening the lives of my children was not going to be tolerated. I told this man that I had no idea who he married or who his children were or aware they lived. But I told him I'd bet you I can find them and I described in intimate graphic details what I would do to his children and his wife should the slightest bit of harm come to my children. I told him I am capable of being just as crazy and brutal and inconsiderate as you are. I turned around to walk away two steps away from this man the Lord stop me. I all of a sudden knew what the Lord wanted to tell this man. I walked back to him and looked him right in the face. I told him that I knew about the six people that they had murdered or had killed through the mob in Pittsburgh. And that God would not let these incidents go without passing judgment on them in this life. I told him that I knew that his dad Johnson was still alive. And I also knew that he was the one that had ordered the execution of six of these people. And in a couple of cases that he had done the dirty work himself. I told Silas to keep a close eye on his father because a judgment that God was about to bring down on him was going to be severe. Beyond your ability to apprehend it.

I told him that his father would not die until his body had experienced considerable decomposition while he was still alive. The rest of his life would be spent in excruciating agony for which there would be no painkiller to abate the pain. I told him that for the rest of your father's life he would suffer pain and agony beyond human comprehension. The stench of your father's rotting flesh will be so bad that not a single human being will be able to come within half a mile of him. I said I want you to see what happens to your father because the same judgment is about to be passed on you as well. I told him some of the people that your father has had killed were blood bought children of the living God. God does not throw his children away to dogs like you.

Chapter 37

Arrest And Conviction With Grace

As a result of this meeting I was set up in an extortion rap and was arrested by the New York State police and imprisoned in Kingston New York. I was taken in front of a judge where bail was set at $45,000 cash or 90,000 real estate. I was imprisoned in Kingston New York for two months. A woman I'd never met before showed up and said that she had $40,000 to put up for my bail. I had already given my attorney $5000. My son Jeremy was with me when the arrest went down. He was released after being held for seven days. The total purpose of my arrest was to have a conviction brought against me for first-degree grand larceny by extortion.

My attorney and myself opted for a trial by judge instead of by a jury. We discovered during the process of these legal proceedings, from outside sources, that the Group of Brothers had already spent over $1 million to have me arrested. They bought some state troopers, a prosecutor, and the judge. The state troopers served their purpose. The prosecutor never tried my case. Another prosecutor was called in. The judge also never served on my case. A judge was called in from retirement to hear my case. During the process of the trial Silas and the other man both lied under oath on the witness stand. My son was never at the trial because my attorney chose not to call him as a witness. I also did not testify on my own behalf. This in hindsight I believe may have been a mistake. The final outcome of this trial was different than Silas had intended and was also somewhat interesting. The purpose was to have me convicted of first-degree grand larceny by extortion. This would carry a sentence of 15 to 20 years. Silas had already bought and paid for someone in jail to put me to death. The judge threw out first-degree grand larceny without any hesitation. As stated that it was absolutely no evidence for that extreme case. He also said that he honestly believed that I had been a fool to try to make a settlement on my own. But I should have called in at least an attorney to assist me. He stated that I had a fool for a client and a greater fool for an attorney. He found me guilty of third-degree grand larceny by extortion as well as fourth degree. The judge was also not a fool. He was well aware that Silas and the other man had both perjured themselves. I was sentenced to time served and five years of probation for which I would have to serve three years. I was also slapped with a five year restraining order preventing me from going near any of the Group of Brothers communities. This restraining order was not going to be very difficult to keep.

Before sentence was passed Heinrich who is now the leader of the Groupof Brothers spoke in court and made a statement before sentencing. He spoke about how I had grown up in the community and how well I had been treated and how they couldn't understand what had just happened. That I had changed so much from the nice little boy that they had raised. The niceness of his statements was enough to make a pig vomit. He also said that they extend forgiveness and pleaded for the judge not to oppose a harsh sentence. He said that in his opinion that I needed psychiatric help and should be confined to a mental institution for a number of years.When it came to my turn to make a statement I was eager to speak. However my attorney was not so eager to allow me to say anything. I chose to speak anyway. In open court I told how the Group of Brothers under the leadership of this man's father, Vonkopf had very nearly destroyed my family, had alienated five of my brothers from the rest of the family. I told how the community had prevented myself in five of my brothers from seeing my parents. How I had been locked up with six Andother children ages six through nine for six months. How I had been locked up in solitary confinement for a month in October and November of the year with no heat and no blankets wearing only a pair of shorts and a T-shirt for one month. I told how I spent a year in slave labor in their factory and how I was now suffering from severe hearing loss because I was not permitted to wear hearing protection while working in their factories.I told the court how I had been excommunicated when I was 13 years old and told point blank never ever to return again that they never wanted to see me. I told about the brutal beating that my brother Ben had suffered at the hands of one of their members. A beating that very nearly left him dead when he was nine years old. Before I finish my story I denounced Heinrich. Heinrich's entire story was nothing more than an outright blatant lie spoken in open court for Your Honor to hear. I denounced his plea for leniency as well as his plea for forgiveness. I told court that there was even now a contract out against me to try to kill me. I told the court that in my honest opinion and from what I know this community and these particular people that their sole purpose was to try to get me into a position where I'd be confined in some way shape or form so that they knew where I was when they wanted to kill me. I told the judge negating everything that Heinrich has said I totally trust your judgment as to the sentence that you want to impose as being just and fair. I told the judge that I knew that in a spirit he knew the real truth of what was really going on here.His judgment had not been clouded by what had been written in papers of how nice and wonderful Christian community this was.I also told the court that these people steal from the local community through the welfare systems and other programs that are available for pregnant women and women with children to the tune of millions of dollars a year. That they do not deserve or need these services.They are extremely rich and make a great deal of money in businesses that they conduct. A lot of their money is siphoned off when cash is paid for their products and is deposited in Swiss bank accounts.The end result of this proceeding was that I was sentenced to time served and three years probation. When I got outside the courtroom Channel 8 news from Hartford Connecticut was waiting for me. They did a half-hour interview on me and I told the truth and answered every question that they asked. In Thomaston Connecticut when I got back home Channel 3 news from New Haven Connecticut was there and set up an interview also a half hour long at which time I again told the absolute truth and answered all their questions. These two interviews ran in their entirety on the evening news in the next few days. This caused a burst of outright anger from people in Connecticut. The Group of Brothers was forced to close their community that they had a Connecticut and move all of their people to New York. The community was also hit with a lawsuit for back taxes for property. The lawsuit stated that they could no longer claim all of their property as tax deductible because it was a part of the church. They were allowed to tax deduct the building in which they actually conduct they worship services.The three years probation I was allowed to serve in Alliance Ohio. I had made a move to Alliance Ohio in the summer of 1996. I served to three years probation during which time I also got an opportunity to counsel some of the probation officers. I also got to meet some very interesting people there working in this field. I also reestablish my business of home remodeling and continued to make a living in this field until March of 2007. During this entire episode with this community I again experienced the protection of the Lord. The leadership of this community has wanted me dead since I was 10 years old. Since this episode my children and myself have been well protected by the hand of God. God's favor once again was clearly seen.

Chapter 38

Melissa's Eye Miracle

In November of 1996 my daughter Melissa had an accident at school. She was snapping a bungee cord down to hold a cage top in place Another girl knocked into her causing her to let go of the bungee cord. The bungee cords snap back and the steel huke struck Melissa in her right eyeball. This caused the retina of her right eye to become totally detached except for by the optic nerve. She was taken to a specialist in Waterbury Connecticut who examined her eye for damage. He performed surgery to repair the detached retina. He opened up her eyeball and went inside the eye and surgically reattached the retina to the back of her eye. He then filled her eyes with an inert gas. As the gas dissipated the eye would again fill with fluid. This seemed to solve the problem. This also caused Melissa to have to wear special corrective lens in that eye. Melissa talked to me about this problem about a year later. She complained that she could not see very well out of her right eye. I asked her how she had survived the other two times she had almost died of medical problems when she was very young. I told her that it was by the grace and mercy of God and the healing hand of the Lord that had been extended to her that had brought her through the crisis. I said let's pray for your right eye. After praying for a right eye the problems seem to become less noticeable.It was some years after this that Melissa went to a different eye doctor. The eye doctor, after hearing what happened to her right eye took photographs of the inside for eye. When he had developed the photographs he informed Melissa that she should not be able to see daylight with that eye. He did not believe that she could really see anything. He covered her left eye witha piece of cloth and then told her to put her hand over the piece of cloth to make sure that her left eye was completely shielded. He then ran some more tests on her right eye. After being convinced that she was really able to see with her right eye, he told her that with the damage in her right eye she should not be able to see even daylight. And he himself said that if she could see anything more than daylight it was a miracle. Melissa informed me of this new eye doctor's examination and what he had discovered. She also told me that with the lenses that he had made for her she could see quite well out of her right eye. I asked her if she was still convinced that she had not been healed. She informed me that she was totally convinced that by the hand of God she had been healed again. And yet once again we have to declare that the favor of God and the grace and mercy of the Lord and the healing hand of God had been extended to my children.

Chapter 39

Healing And God's Preservation

I found an apartment in Alliance Ohio. I also started advertising to get my remodeling business back on the road. I was able to secure enough work to make ends meet but it was slim pickings. But I got enough work to make a living. In the fall of 1997 I was doing some work helping my uncle in his business. He had established a small business where he remodeled cars that had previously been damaged in accidents that he bought from insurance companies. He then later resold these automobiles after they had been restored. He had a junkyard in back of his home. I started helping him pull motors out of these wrecked cars and strip off other useful parts so that he could juke the rest of the car. In the process of doing this, the fifth vertebrae in my back again broke and was causing excruciating pain. In October of 1997 on a Sunday afternoon I was laying in bed trying to sleep. But the pain in my back was so severe that I could do little but cry. I finally cried out to the Lord for healing for my back.Remove the pain thatis so bad that I didn't think I could tolerate it anymore. Immediately my back moved back and forth and up and down and popped a few times and went straight. The pain was now completely gone. I was so exhausted because I hadn't slept in five or six days. I went to sleep and didn't wake up until Monday afternoon at 3 PM. I had slept for 24 hours. I got up and walked around for an hour before I realized there was no pain in my back. When I felt my back there was a tender spot where the vertebrae had been broken. Other than that I had no pain at all in my back. I have never experienced any pain in my back since then. I was completely and told he healed.

From the summer of 1996 on I made continual trips every other weekend to Connecticut to see my children. On most weekends I spent about a half a day with my children. By the fall of 1997 it seemed like my kids were very busy with their own lives and the most I got to see them was for an hour or hour and a half on a weekend. This did not seem like much of a reward for driving 8 ½ hours each way to see tham. The problem I had at this point was to come up with enough money to pay for the trip.But it was on one of the last trips that I made to Connecticut that my life once again was threatened. It was in the fall of 1997. I was driving a1964 Oldsmobile Delta 88 diesel that I had borrowed from my uncle. The car ran very well and I had used it for several trips to Connecticut. On this particular trip going to Connecticut was not a problem. On the way back I noticed I was being followed starting in western New Jersey. As I came into Pennsylvania I notice not one car but two cars were following me. I wasn not going to tolerate this for a very long. I put the gas pedal to the floor and maxed out the car. Flat out this car would do 98 miles an hour. I put it in the left lane and just held my foot to the floor for some 20 minutes. The cars in back of me were staying right with but were staying a couple hundred feet behind. I finally got tired of this game and stopped suddenly in the left lane. Traffic at this point was not very heavy but there were a few cars. When the car stopped I jumped out and put my hand inside my jacket as if I was carrying a gun. I motioned to do two boys in the cars behind me with my hand to bring them closer. At this point I stepped closer to the back of the car. Because it was in the left lane the first car made a left turn and went across the little valley in the medium and went back into the eastbound lane. The car in the center lane made a right turn and went off the road through the fence and onto a side road and went east.The rest of that trip back to Ohio was uneventful. But I reminded myself that I would have to be a little bit more diligent and continually look over my shoulder. It was in the summer of 1998 that I found out through outside sources the a contract had been put out against me through Pittsburgh to try to kill me. But killing me was supposed to look like a traffic accident. The man that told us about this said that he was in on a meeting in a hotel room in Pittsburgh at 11 o'clock at night. He was with Siluse, and another man in a dark hotel room. He told us that the only topic of conversation he and Siluse had with this man from Pittsburgh was the demise and elimination of David Maendel.

I knew then that every single time I went to Connecticut would be a problem.

In September or October of 1998 I came home to my apartment after being with somebody that I cared a great deal about. There were also some other things that were really bothering me like this attempt on my life. I came into my apartment and lay facedown on the rug. I cried out to the Lord about the problems I was facing. For 45 minutes I stayed in prayer. There was apparently no answer at the moment so I went to get up. In a half raised position the Lord showed me a vision. In the vision I found myself in the desert. I was walking through the desert holding my father's hand. But in the vision I was only a child. This desert was extremely dry. The cactus all around us were shriveled and wrinkled and completely dried up and almost totally lifeless. My father looked down at me and said "I want you to keep your eyes open there something in his desert I want you to find". My response was that there couldn not possibly be anything here. This desert is so dead and dried up there is nothing here. He said to me"keep your eyes open as we walk". We walked up a slight incline. When we got to the top of this little hill and started down the other side, I noticed something glittering in the sand about 10 feet in front of us. I pulled out my father's hand and ran up and scooped up what looked like a rock. It was a marquis shaped gem about 3 inches longer than my hand. At the widest point it was about 4 inches wide. At the thickest point in the center it was about 3 ½ inches thick. I rubbed it to try to get some of the grime and dirt off it. But as hard as I rubbed I couldn't make any progress in removing the dirt. I came back and gave it to my father. He took it in his hand and started rubbing it with his thumb. The tenderness and loving kindness of his thumb rubbing the stone I have never witnessed before. He very gently and tenderly kept rubbing it untill a part of the of the gem started to come clean. He handed it back to me. He said that I had to caress this with tenderness and loving-kindness untill shown its absolute most brilliant luster then I had to give it back to him. I looked at the stone when he gave it back to me and the part that he had cleaned off. The stone was a deep translucent red. And at that instant I knew that this stone had almost no value in dollars and cents but it was precious beyond my ability to comprehend. It took me till 2005 before I understood what this vision meant.

Chapter 40

Visions And God's Presence Increases

In the middle of September 1998 the Assemblies of God church I was going to had scheduled a baptism by submersion. This baptism was to take place towards the end of November of 1998. I had never been baptized by immersion. I really wanted to experience this process. I was reading everything Scripture about water baptism and try to prepare myself for a wonderful encounter. It was during this period of about six weeks that the Lord started to speak to me about the hate and bitterness that I carried all my life. The Lord told me that this hate and bitterness had to be laid aside. The people that have done these injustices to me he would have to take care of himself. At first I was very reluctant because I had hated this way since I was 10 or 11 years old. I even reminded the Lord that I hatedthe same things he hated. I hated for the same reason that he hated. I tried to justify my hate in the hearing of the Lord God. Finally the Lord got my attention and convinced me that I had to lay the hate aside. He reminded me that he could not use me for the purpose that he had brought me this far for if I did not lay my hate aside. It took me a while to do this but with the help of the Holy Spirit it was finally made possible.The incredible relief that I experienced and also the tremendous weight that was taken off my shoulders from having carried this burden all my life. The baptism that I was to be a part of was scheduled for last week in November, I believe there were four of us going to be baptized. When it came my turn to be baptized I was given a chance to make a confession to the congregation. All of us were given this opportunity and we all took it. I told the congregation that I've been a Christian all of my life. But that I had never been baptized by immersion. And that I believed that it says in the Bible that this was a necessary part of our salvation. When I was baptized the pastor dunked me underwater and in the name of the Father Son and Holy Spirit he baptized me. I went into the water one way and came out different. I was so completely and totally transformed that I did not recognize myself. It took three or four months for me to get used to the way I now was. This baptism completely and totally revolutionized and changed my life and me from that point on.

A few months after this, on a Sunday afternoon I was laying down taking a nap, trying to. I couldn't sleep and after about an hour I went to get up out of bed. Again In a half race position the Lord stopped me. The Lord showed me another vision. In the vision I was standing on a street of translucent material that had a yellow tinge to it. Apparently gold. To my left was a river, and on each bank of the river were fruit trees, this was the river of life. I know now where I was I was in heaven. To my right were houses too numerous to count even if I had the time. These mansions were gorgeous beyond anyone's wildest imagination. On the edge of the street in front of each mention was a mailbox. The mailboxes were all the same. The post of the mailbox was about 3 inches square and was the color of royal blue marbled and periled. The mailboxes were the same color. The posts were trimmed with gold on the corners end had gold lettering on the mailboxes was. A long ways in front of me I noticed that there was a name on one of the mailboxes. But I could not see what the name was, so I walked up closer to the mailbox. I saw that the name on the mailbox was my name. At first I kind of thought that this was a sign that the Lord was going to take me home that my work here on earth was finished. I became overjoyed and started to sing. But then I thought the Lord has never shown me a vision that would give me any indication that this would benefitme personally so much. So I paid a little closer attention. Up ahead of me almost ½ a mile away there was a bridge that went over the river. People were going back and forth across this bridge and on the other side of the riverbank there were people walking back and forth. But nobody seemed to be paying any attention to me or even notice that I was there. It was at this point that the vision ended. I knew almost immediately that this vision had something to do with the vision I had just a few months before. The vision were I found the stone in the desert. But again I was at a loss of what this vision meant. It would be 2005 before I finally put the two visions together and understood them clearer.

In June of 2000 I went to see a doctor because I have pain in my belly that was obviously due to a urinary tract infection. The doctor came in and examined me and told me that I had a urinary track infection. He also took a blood sample to see with my blood count was. He prescribed antibiotic, but he thought that he had prescribed it for two months, but he had only given me two weeks worth. He made an appointment to see me again in two weeks time. When I went back in two weeks he asked me if I was still taking antibiotics. I told him they ran out yesterday that he had only given me two weeks worth. He told me that the blood test had shown the highest blood count he had ever seen in his life for a man that was still alive. He said there was absolutely no doubt in his mind that I had prostate cancer. He explained that maybe my blood count was unusually high to start with. But he said that this high a blood count definitely indicates prostate cancer. This was on a Tuesday afternoon. He told me that he wanted to put me in a hospital on Monday morning for surgery. I thanked the doctor very much and told him I wasn not going to be in the hospital on Monday morning that he could operate on whomever else he could find and I went home. The urinary tract infection had gone away but I still had pain in my belly. I also had other problems. From the time I was nine years old with the Group of Brothers I had been getting severe migraine headaches. I had these headaches for 3 to 5 days a week. And sometimes they were so severe that I was totally nonfunctional. But I had developed a high-level tolerance to pain. And most of the time I could live with it.In December of 2000 I guess I was in a state of bad depression. My home remodeling business was not going that well. There were also a large number of unanswered questions that I was continually seeking the Lord about and apparently did not get an answer. I knew that something was going on in the spiritual realm that I just could not get a grip on. I also knew that it was not God's fault.There was something wrong in my approach to the problems I was having. During this period of time I also cried out to Lord to make his healing hand available to me to help solve some of the physical problems that I had. The Lord's compassion opened up to mycalling and descended on me like I had never experienced it before. One of the major problems I had at the time was an irregular heartbeat. It seemed to affect me most when I was lying down. My heart would go from a normal heartbeat and would raise extremely high. I could feel my blood pressure building at this point. Then without warning my heart would stop. It would stop for one or 2 or 3 or sometimes 4 beats and then come back to a normal heartbeat. On several occasions my pulse completely stopped for what seemed like six or seven heartbeats. At this point I had to hit myself in the chest with my fist and my heart would start beating again. But during one of these episodes I decided not to do anything. And simply told the Lord that I was not going to start my heart again that I was coming home. This again did not agree with where the Lord was taking me. In order to do the work the Lord was preparing me for I had to actually be alive. I finally hit myself in the chest with my fist and my heart resumed a normal pulse. At that moment however I was healed of the irregular heartbeat and never experienced it again.It was from the month of December 2000 until the end of 2001 that I experienced a great number of episodes of instant healing of some major defects and my health. Prostate cancer I had been diagnosed with completely disappeared. Migraine headaches completely disappeared and I have never ever had them since. Excruciating hemorrhoids that I've had most of my life went away. I also discovered that my pancreas had completely redeveloped. I no longer had any problem with anything I wanted eat. I also had a slipped disc in my lower back was giving me problems this was also healed.The Lord was so very powerfully present in my life and in my being that I started to pay attention. I knew that there was something going on. I knew that God was prepairing me for a special purpose. God's word says that he doesn't favor any of us above anyone else, He treats us all equally. So what is it that was so special about me that caused him to favor me in such a wonderful way? I didnot know the answer to these questions. I did however learn to pay a lot closer attention to things in the spirit. My constant prayer to the Lord was that he would open my spirit to be able to have greater spiritual discernment and that my spiritual senses would start being developed so that I could both see hear and understand spiritual matters. I also prayed that when the Lord spoke to me that he would guard me and protect me against being able to hear false information from demonic sources. These are prayers that were answered in a fantastic way almost immediately. The Lord continued to show me things that were coming for the church. Also where the church had to be in preparation for Christ to come back to take the church out of the world. It became very clear to me that some dramatic changes in both the church and our personal lives as Christians had to take place if we were going to fit into the plan God had for us. I determine for myself that I would pursue a greater interest and pursuit of spiritual principles and concepts. And to make a greater effort to keep myself available at all times to hear a word from my God. Thesehealings that I experienced since December of 2000 again was a very obvious display of God's favor. The Lord had once again touch my body in such a tremendous and powerful way I had been healed of problems that I had experienced since I was eight or ten years old.

Chapter 41

Attempts On my life Continue

In 2002 I made the purchase of the 1998 Pontiac Grand Prix. It was a neat little car and got very good gas mileage. This car was especially fun to drive to Connecticut. It was quite stable on the road and was comfortable to sit in for long periods of time. Again I was going to Connecticut at least one weekend a month to see my children. I was also getting into the habit of calling them a couple of weeks in advance to plan a weekend. By doing this I found that I had a chance of at least spending half a day with both of them. It was on one of these weekends that I again encountered a taile. Someone was following me. It was a very new Cadillac Escalade That was white in color. I discovered this car following me in New Jersey on the way back from Connecticut. When I discovered the taile it was about six or seven o'clock in the evening. I did not do anything about it I just kept a close eye on it and kept on driving. I wanted to see if the guy kept following me. About 100 miles into Pennsylvania I got off an exit at a truck stop to get some fuel. But I lingered at the truck stop. The Escalade followed me off the exit. It also parked at the truck stop and waited. The Windows on this Escalade were very dark and I could not see inside. I got back into my car and got back on interstate 80 but instead of going west I got on the on ramp to go east. The Escalade followed me. I went off an exit and turned around and came back. The Escalade was still on my tail. I started to drive a little faster and to keep my pace up and to try to dodge in and out of traffic. But traffic was relatively light.The other problem was a fog was starting to set in that was apparently going to be very widespread. The Escalade followed me almost all away across Pennsylvania but made no move against me. At exit 5, which is just 45 miles from the Ohio line I got off the exit again. I did not need gas I had enough to get home. When I got down to the bottom of the exit ramp I went straight across and got back on the on ramp at which point I turned off my headlights. By this time the fog was so heavy that you could not see 5 feet in front of the car.It was also about 2:00 AM.And it was almost impossible to see the road looking out the side window of the Grand Prix. The car I had was also a dark blue.So I was sure that the Escalade would not see me. I got back up on interstate 80 and put my foot floor on the accelerator. My Grand Prix would do 105 miles an hour flat out. I just prayed that the Lord would hide me and keep me on the road until I got home. I was watching the centerline on the road out the side window. I didn't turn the headlights on again until I crossed the Ohio line. I managed to lose the Escalade at exit 5. I also understood by this time that the Lord is keeping me safe.

It was about this time that the prophetic abilities that I've had since I was eight years old started to increase in both usefulness and frequency. I was discovering that the Lord a lot more often used me for both personal prophecy as well as corporate prophecy in a church setting. I also found it very interesting that a lot of people were not interested in a Prophet of God coming to them and informing them of what it was the Lord wanted them to know. One of the most common reactions that I've experienced in my life is," if the Lord wants me to know something he'll find a way to give me the information". My reaction to that was to tell them that's why I was theregiving them the information God sent me to give them. But for some reason that was never quite good enough. And it puzzled me what do they expect that Jesus Christ is going to come to them in person to show them the nail prints in his hands and feet to prove that he had been sent by God.To give them a little tiny bit of clarification in a troubled life. Wasn't it sufficient that God had sent one of his messengers? I guess not.

Chapter 42

Visions Continue

It was in early fall of 2003 and I was at home in the early evening hours. The Lord showed me a vision when I was wide-awake so I know that this was not a dream. I have also learned after seeing many visions what the difference is between a vision and dream. In this vision I found myself in the woods. But these were not any ordinary woods. The smallest tree was 2 feet in diameter. The size of the trees went as high as 4 feet in diameter. The other thing I noticed immediately was that there was no underbrush on the forest floor there were no weeds, no briars, and no brambles. The forest floor was almost as clean as a floor in your living room and I was beginning to admire the beautiful woods. Up ahead of me a few hundred feet I saw a strange animal coming out from behind one of the big trees. This animal had the face of the pig with a snout of a pigand tasks that went both up and down. It had the feet of the pig but also had horns. The front half of his body had hair and the back half was entirely hairless. The eyes of this pig were like orange burning coals, and smoke was coming out of his nostrils. As this beast came towards me I, without thinking, reached over my shoulder with my right hand and pulled out a sword that I was carrying on my back. At first as I held his sword out straight in front of me I was thinking that this sword is awfully dirty. Like I had not cared for it but it was different dirt. This sword was dirty from having been used a lot. I had not had time to clean it from previous battles. As I held this sword out straight in front of me the beast in front of me stopped. But at the same time I noticed that there was another beast just like it but smaller coming up behind me. As I stood sideways and held this sword straight out in front of me the two beasts stopped and just glared at me. The beast in back of me was exactly the same as the beast in front of me only smaller. At this moment the vision ended. It was about six months before the Lord explained the meaning of this vision. Three clock one morning after I'd been praying for enlightenment for a considerable length of time the Lord woke me. He told me that the beast in back of me represented the persecution that I had suffered all of my life. And he said the beast in front of me represents the persecution that you will still have to endure to perform the service that I've prepared you for. But the Lord told me you "have all the necessary weapons that you need to get to where I'm sending you". And he said "I would never leave you or forsake you I will always be with you and you have nothing to fear". This was not only reassuring but it brought me back to the realization that the Lord was indeed preparing me for service sometime in the future. But what I was allowed to do now in the churches was actually training me and preparing me for what was coming later.In the spring of 2004 I was sitting in a church in Louisville Ohio. It was during a normal Sunday morning worship service. And it happened like somebody had changed the channel on the TV. I was standing outside on a hill. The Lord spoke to me and said "I want you to look in the sky to the east. And tell me what it is you see". And I said "Lord I see a very small cloud". And he said "keep your eye on the cloud". And I noticed that as the cloud came closer it grew larger and larger. When it was almost overhead I noticed that the Lord Jesus was in the middle of the cloud. I also noticed that the cloud was not white or black it was beautiful pastel colors, colors of the rainbow. And the Lord spoke to me and he said "I will bring a new rain on the church. The kind of rain the church has never experienced before. I will pour out my Spirit on all of my people and transform them to become the bride of Christ. So that when the Lord Jesus returns to take his bride home that my church will be ready". This vision was an incredible revelation because I had been praying for a long time how would the church become the bride of Christ without spot or wrinkle when the Lord comes back to get it.

In 2004 after repeatedly seeking the Lord in prayer and asking him what it was that he was preparing me for I finally received an answer. It had been very obvious to me since the Lord called in my marker in September of 1992 that the Lord was preparing me for a specific purpose. In December of 2004 the Lord gave me an answer. He spoke to me and told me what it is that he is preparing me for. I was shocked and disputed with the Lord for about six months. This is not me Lord I can not do this, there is no way. About five months later in May of 2005 the Lord woke me out of a sound sleep at 2:00 AM. This was not a gentle awakening he shook my whole bed. He told me "don't you ever talk to me like this again. Before you were conceived in your mother's belly I knew you. The moment you were conceived I spoke your spirit into existence pre-programmed for this very purpose. I called you from the womb to be my profit. My Holy Spirit has been with you since the moment you were conceived. My presence has never left you it has been with you always. I will never leave you and I will give you the ability to perform the service that I prepared you to perform". This was the harshest rebuke I had ever received from any living entity in my life. My father was a shoemaker when I was a young child and I would rather be rebuke with a piece of leather than the rebuke I had just received. From now on I want to be extremely careful not to raise a doubting question with the Lord again. I also made up my mind that from now on I would make a greater effort to concentrate on believing what the Lord told me. I made up my mind to allow God to be God, and I was going to concentrate on being David hopefully a truly humble servant of the Lord. I was also going to pay better attention to what the Lord was doing with me overall and to where he was taking me. I was paying too much attention to the problems that I was experiencing and not paying enough attention to the answer or the solution.It was at about this time in my life that I started to notice a significant change in my relationship with the Lord. I did not understand this change at first. It took me almost a year to understand what truly had happened. Once someone is born again they experience a spiritual rebirth. At this point they become sons or daughters of the living God. In our relationship with God the Holy Spirit brings us to a more intimate relationship with the Lord by taking us to different levels. Each level we attain is higher than the one we just came off of. I had seen my progress increase on different levels over the previous 10 or 12 years. The level that the Lord had just brought me to was a level that I did not know existed. This new level was a level of

Son Ship. This new level also allowed me to have a more intimate contact with the Lord. It also allowed me to have a more intimate access to the Lord. I found that I was receiving an answer to prayer almost before my prayer was finished. The Lord started to a part answers to my prayer directly into my spirit. I was also becoming increasingly aware that I had a more direct access to the answers in my spirit. Access to information and revelation was also more readily available to me.

The other thing that I started noticing was that spiritual encounters were becoming more frequent. Always being used in different ways by the Holy Spirit. Gifts that I knew that I had had for many years were starting to show up and the Holy Spirit was starting to sharpen them and use them in a powerful way. One of the things that developed during the time with the Group of Brothers, especially during the times of interrogation, was a gift to be able to see people spirit. This also involved, to a lesser degree being able to read people's mind. This came into play in a powerful way when I was asked to go take down the TV tower at the home of a pastor from Louisville. I took the TV tower down but knew that there was another reason why I was there. When the pastor came out of his house I asked him why I was at his home. He said well to take my TV tower down. I said that I understood that and I said there is another reason why I'm here. I asked him what was going on in his life. And he started telling me about his wife who had been semi—comatose for about three years. I said that's the reason I'm here I was sent to talk to Mary. He said "how did you know her name" I said "the Lord just told me. I said "she is at the Alliance Hospital". He said that was correct that he would go to see her Monday afternoon at about 4:00 PM. I said that at four o'clock in the afternoon I would meet him there.When I arrived at the hospital room the pastor was already there and was talking to his wife. And he introduced me to Marry. I asked faster to please let me go up to stand by her head so I could talk to her. And he told me "while she's in a coma talking to her does not do much good". I said "I'm a man of God the Lord has sent me not only to talk to Mary but also to communicate with her". He was awfully skeptical. I sat down in his chair right by Mary's face. I said "Mary my name is David". And this woman became quite agitated and started moving around in bed. I toldMary she should relax. I said "the Lord has sent me to communicate with you". I said "the Lord has heard your prayer. He has never been very far away from you. He has always been with you. And he knows that since you've been in this state that you're in now that you have become very discouraged. You can't figure out why the Lord has left you in this state. You also can't figure out why the Lord has sidelined you from being an assistant in your husband's Ministry and affecting lives". I said "the Lord wants you to know that in the present condition that you're in now you have reached a great many people for the Lord. He wants you to know that every single moment of every day that you are affecting people for Christ. He wants you to know that you are a powerful witness in a state you are in. You knew from the beginning of your Christian walk that therewould be persecution and hardships. Because those hardships, occurred in a different way than you had envisioned, does not mean that the Lord has neglected you in anyway. I'm supposed to tell you that you should change your outlook and allow the peace and joy of the Lord to fill your presence. Your ministry is not yet finished there are still people that you have to witness to. And just because you can't talk to them does not mean that you are not witnessing to them". I said "Mary be at peace and praise God in your spirit that he has not let go of you and that he is still using you in ministering to people every single day. Ask him to forgive you for your unbelief, make things right with him. He is the force by which we exist and have our being". After this powerful witness by the Lord through me to this comatose woman her disposition totally changed. Her husband told me afterwards that she again had the joy in her that, she always had before she went comatose. The Lord was not only showing his grace and mercy and his favorite but he was also allowing me to serve him with the gifts that he had given me. And it was making a difference in people's lives. I also needed a sign to show me that I was still useful to the Lord. That I was still serving an important purpose instead of just existing. I had just been given all the sign that I need.

Chapter 43

VX 1900 Strata Liner

In June of 2006 I purchased a brand-new Yamaha motorcycle it was a VX 1900 Strata Liner cruiser. When I first bought this motorcycle I took a trip to Connecticut with it. The trip to Connecticut was a wonderful trip. I absolutely enjoyed riding a motorcycle and being out in the open air and being able to feel and see God's creation. I spent a Saturday and Sunday in Connecticut and no Monday morning drove back to Ohio. I had gotten about halfway across the state of Pennsylvania on Interstate 80 when I noticed that an old pickup truck was following me extremely close. This pickup truck was only about 20 feet in back of me at 75 miles an hour. I crack the throttle a little bit and less than 2 seconds I was doing 95. But the pickup truck kept pace with me without losing any ground. This may have looked like an old pickup truck but what he had under the hood was not old. This pickup truck had been set up to be a hard runner. I picked up a little more speed but he stayed right with me. This time to show me what he could really do he got less than 5 feet in back of me. This man very obviously wanted to cause an accident that would kill me. I decided I'd had enough of this I speed up to 140 miles an hour. I was absolutely sure that my motorcycle would top 200 if necessary. At 140 miles an hour I was pulling away from this old pickup truck quite rapidly. It was very obvious that he could not stay with me at this speed. I held 140 miles an hour for the next 75 miles. Traffic was very light and the road was in very good shape. When I got to an exit where there was a gas station I got off the exit and went to the gas station and hid my bike behind the building so that he could not see me. I never saw the pickup truck again after that. The Lord had shown me once again that he was always with me to watch over me and to protect me. Yet again the Lord had shown me favor.

In 2005 and 2006 I was doing a lot of the vinyl siding. I was working with a young man a high school senior who I met in church. This young man was doing a great job for me. However I had to be the one to do all the climbing as high as 35 of 40 feet in the air. These siding jobs extended over into January, February of 2007. I finished the last siding job that I had on the second Friday in February of 2007. At 1:30 PM I came home to my house. I open the door and stepped inside. Just inside the door the Lord stopped me. He said to me "within the next six weeks there will be another attempt on your life. This next attempt will be very nearly fatal. But you have to remember who I am and who you are". I was very shaken. That evening after I knew that my son in Connecticut had gotten home from work I called him. In a highly emotional voice I started talking to him. He stopped me and asked me "dad, what in the world is wrong". I told them that the Lord had just informed me that within the next six weeks there would be another attempt on my life. I told him that when he heard that I'd been killed or am dying not to believe it. But that he should instead get his sister and get into his car and come to Canton Ohio, to Altman Hospital, and come into my room and asked me that I would be there.

On March 30, 2007 I was finishing up a small job for a friend of mine. I got back home to the house at 1:00 PM. I got my new Yamaha motorcycle out and went for a ride. It was a beautiful machine and it was a great deal of fun to ride it. March 30, 2007 was a beautiful, sunny, warm day. I went for a ride. I never stopped to think that this day was exactly 6 weeks after the Lord spoken to me on the second Friday in February. I went out to State Street inAlliance Ohio and went east. At the intersection of State St. and Homework road a car to my right pulled out and wanted to go west. I saw the car coming and went this far to my left as I could to avoid a collision. The car came all the way across the road and hit me broadside. The accident took my right foot off of my leg starting at the back of the leg just above the ankle. The cut went down the right side through my ankle and across the top of my foot all the way to my instep. My foot was hinged by a piece of flesh on the back left side of my heel. The bottom half of my leg had been turned 90° to the right of the top half of my leg. My knee had been completely torn out except for the large tendent and on the back. The only thing I had left of my ankle was my Achilles tendon. A young man at a gas station right there saw the accident and recognized me as the man who was injured. He came over and sat astride of my belly and held onto my leg just above the knee. I was bleeding profusely from the wound of my foot having been removed. An ambulance was called and when they arrived their refuse to touch me. Instead they called a life flight helicopter to be flown in from Canton Ohio. When the helicopter arrived they put me on a stretcher and put me into the helicopter. I remember being put into the back of this big yellow helicopter. Halfway to Altman hospital I apparently died.The girl who was a paramedic fought hard to keep me alive. At Altman hospital four doctors worked on me for 2 ½ hours to stabilize me so that they could operate. Twice in that period of time they covered me with a sheet and wheeled me to the morgue. They told me afterwards that I was stone cold dead and had absolutely no life signs both times. I was awakened in surgery. I asked the doctor where we were and he said we were in emergency surgery. So I asked why he wasn't operating. He told me that they had forgotten to get me to sign a piece of paper. When I asked him what the paper was he told me that it gives them the right to amputate my right leg 6 inches below the knee. I asked them to do me a favor. He asked me what I need it. I asked him to please hold up their hands. The three of them held up their hands. I told them that in these three pairs of hands there was more skill than in any thousand other doctors in the hospital combined. And if you think that you came by that skill all by yourself you're badly mistaken. My heavenly Father gave that skill to you for just such a moment is this. Why don't you go ahead and put the foot back on and if you forget where the parts go my heavenly Father is standing right behind you just look over your right shoulder and asking and he will tell you. The doctor told me that there were no parts left to put back together. He told me that my ankle was completely gone. My response was go ahead and put the foot back on and do your part and the Lord Jesus will take over after you have done what you are supposed to do. They operated for 2 ½ hours to reattach my foot to my leg. They put a steel plate on the right side to hold my foot to my leg.

After 2 ½ hours of surgery they came out of the operating room and told my aunt who was waiting outside "when the infection sets into his leg is going to kill him because I can't get the leg off fast enough to save his life". But the doctor said "that's a decision that he has already made.He won't let me take a leg off 6 inches below the knee". I was in the hospital for 18 days. My children showed up on the third day to see me. I vaguely remember them because I was on a double dose of morphine. The nurses cared for me extremely well. I was now a celebrity. After having died in the emergency room twice I was still alive and they could not understand why.I started to question the Lord about what had gone wrong. I met the Lord at 2:00 AM on April 10. I was standing in a greenfield.In the back left and corner of the green field was an oak tree that was about 4 feet in diameter with spreading branches. Under the oak tree there were thousands of little children. The Lord stood in front of me and looked at me for about five minutes without saying a word. He then turned around and walked away. When he got away about 20 feet he turned and faced the me. The question was still on my face. He spread out his hands and asked me" who was it that said you had died. Was it the doctors in this hospital? When will you believe me? I told you that this accident was going to be very nearly fatal." He held out his right hand in front of him. And he said "I hold your life in my hand and if I don't lay your life down he cannot take it from you. And I am not laying your life down". At this point the Lord turned and walked away and I found myself back in the hospital room in excruciating pain. There was a button on the IV system connected to my arm. If I push this button it would inject morphine into my system. I pushed the button three times.

My recovery was to be long and difficult. After 18 days in the hospital I was moved to a nursing home in Alliance Ohio. I was going to spend two months in this nursing home learning how to walk and to strengthen my leg sufficiently so that it would carry my weight. I visited the doctor on a number of occasions because I had a cast on my leg. It was during these visits that he told me what had happened in the emergency room and in surgery. He was one of the doctors that attended me in the emergency room. I asked him if he could do me a favor and he say "sure what is it". And I asked him if he was a Christian and he said yes. I said "I need you to declare this leg a miracle". He got pale and he told me "you could declare the leg whatever you want to. Your miracle is the fact that you're alive. You died twice on us in the emergency room and twice we covered you with a sheet andwheeled you to the morgue. That is your real miracle". I got out of the nursing home at the end of July.I really wanted to go see the 18-year-old young lady who had been driving the car that had hit me. But the Lord was not yet allowing it. By this time I was walking with a cane but with great difficulty. Every step I took my right knee, would separate and tare the cartilage. In the first week of September I was driving around when the Lord spoke to me and told me he wanted me to go see the young lady. I knew where they lived so I drove up into their driveway. There was a man standing by a pickup truck. I asked him if he was her father. He said no I'm her stepfather. At that point her mother came out of the house and told me I could get out of the truck. I looked at her and said "I could be a terrorist you don't even know who I am". She looked at me and said that she knew who I was that I was David Maendel and that they had been waiting for me for four months. I got out of the car and she went back in the house a few minutes later she came back out with a young girl on her left arm. The young lady was sobbing and trying to hide behind her mother. I walked up in front of this young lady and asked her if she was Sharon. She said yes I am and I said I am David Maendel. From 5 feet away this young lady launched herself at me and grab me around the stomach. With her head on my shoulder crying her eyes out she said to me, "I thought I'd kill you I thought I'd killed you". I told her that she had I said that I'd been dead three times but I told her that I'm up I'm alive and I'm walking. I told her that she had to get over this you have a long life ahead of you and you have to get a grip on yourself and learn how to live and how to love again. I held this young lady in my arms for what seemed like 10 minutes. I said that I would have come to see them much sooner but that I needed the insurance money to pay the medical bills. I said I have absolutely nothing against you. You were just in the wrong place and at the wrong time when the devil used you to try to kill me. This accident had a lot less to do with you that it had to do with me. I said I totally completely forgive you and I know that you are not completely free of this but if you give it time the Lord willheal you. After this incident we met quite a few times and each time it was quite apparent that this young lady was going to fully recover. I also realized that her recovery was extremely important to my own healing. This incident showed me very clearly that the enemy was working extremely hard to try to destroy me. But the Lord God himself was working just as hard to protect me and to keep me alive. This entire episode also showed very clearly that the Lord had again shown the extreme favor. The healing of my leg was only made possible because of a number of miracles that happened in the process.

In September of 2007 I had come home to my house from visiting a friend. My knee was extremely sore from walking.My ankle also hurt considerably. I could not walk up the stairs and step up with my right leg. I prayed that the Lord would do something with my right leg so that the knee would not separate. The tendon on the front of my knee had broken loose and was a lump in my shin. Over the period of a half-hour that tendon that was a lump in my shin crawled up my leg and reattached itself to the front of my kneecap. Now I could walk without my knees separating. God's healing hand is awesome.

Chapter 44

"Go To Israel To Meet Someone"

In August of 2007 I was home resting. The Lord showed me a vision. In the vision I was in a building with five or six other people. I was sitting on the couch with two people. One person was in the kitchen and another person was sitting across the coffee table from me in a chair. The man that was sitting in the chair was making fun of me and taunting me. The two that were sitting on the couch with me were laughing at his fun making and thought it was good fun. I however became upset and asked him to please stop. This only made them increase their fun making of me. In a moment of anger I picked up a glass ashtray and threw it at him. The ashtray never hit this guy it went right through him. In that moment I realized that these characters were not people but were demon spirits. I jumped off the couch and with the name of Jesus kept them away from me. It was at this point that the demons from upstairs came down. They formed a circle around me and tried to get at me. They could not come any closer to me than where they were. This is where the vision ended. On the second Sunday of September a young man by the name of Danny asked me to go to a church that he was a pastor of down in Orrville Ohio. I had met Danny at the church that I was now attending. He had been made a pastor and assign to this church about six months before. I went to church with this young man and on the way down told him about the vision that I had. When we walked into his church I realized that this was the building that I had been in the vision. I told Danny this. He also admitted that things in the church were extremely strained. I told him that I could understand why if therewere six demons hiding in his church. I suggested that we take some time on that Sunday morning and do some spiritual housecleaning. He allowed me to teach the small congregation of 10 people how to evict demons. After teaching them how to evict demons I instructed them to spread out in the church and to go into every single room and in Jesus name order these demons to leave. When we finished there was a noticeable change in the atmosphere of that church as well as the attitude of the congregation. I continued to attend his church from time to time to try to be some assistance to Danny. I had extensive spiritual insight that he needed to develop.On one of these occasions on Wednesday night on the drive home we became involved in a considerable conversation. While talking to Danny the Lord stopped me and started talking to me in my spirit. Danny while driving notices the change in me. I wanted to know what was going on I just held up one finger on my left hand indicating that I needed a few minutes. The Lord said to me "I want you to make arrangements to go to Israel". He further instructed me that I was a Jew of the tribe of Judah. And that I was of the house of David. I relayed this information to Danny. Danny immediately was informed by the Holy Spirit what it was the Lord was preparing me for. He told me what the Holy Spirit is just told him. This confirmation had now come from three different people.

Towards the end of October of 2007 I started doing some research on what the best way was to get to Israel. A pastor of the Assemblies of God church and Alliance Ohio had taken a group to Israel in the past. I went to him and inquired as to how I could get on a tour group to get to Israel. He gave me the telephone number and name of travel agency in New York City to call. I called the travel agency and they told me what it was going to cost. The price included airfare, hotel rooms, and a buffet breakfast, and a buffet dinner. This is just what I needed. I immediately signed up for the next tour, which would be leaving the international airport in New Jersey on March 22 of 2008. I made my down payment by credit card with this travel agency. Over the next month I paid the balance due and was told that I would be going with a tour group from a church in Matthew West Virginia. I was also told that I should be at the airport in New Jersey by 12:30 PM on March 22 of 2008.

I immediately made arrangements to get a passport. I was told that the passport probably wouldn't get to me for about six weeks. That would be cutting it little bit close. However I received my passport within 10 days. The Lord was definitely starting to clear obstacles that were in the way.

Two days before my flight was to depart New Jersey, I drove myself to Connecticut where my son lived. He had agreed to take me to the airport in New Jersey on his way to work in Darien Connecticut. But I was going to have to get to the airport by 10 o'clock in the morning. That wasn't so bad I, have a four-hour wait instead of two hours. I got to the airport by 10:00 AM. I got checked in and was told where I had to wait to go through Israeli security to get on the EL/AL airplane. I had quite a bit of time to wait but at about one o'clock the Israeli security people showed up. They set up six podiums in a row. They called the passengers in one at a time and asked them a dozen questions. When it came my turn to go up to the podium I went up and was asked questions by young woman. The questions were fairly benign but gave them a good idea whether I was going to pose a problem or not. I was quite quickly cleared. I then proceeded down the line to have my luggage x-rayed and to go through a metal detector. I pass security with no problem. I had taken my cane with me because I knew that walking was going to be somewhat of a problem for me. The plane trip to Israel was a wonderful ride. Israeli hospitality began on the airplane. The food was extremely good the hostesses were very helpful and the plane ride itself was almost uneventful. I had gotten to meet the pastor from the church from Matthew West Virginia and he was a very personable man. His wife and granddaughter also accompanied us and we became friends almost immediately. He asked me a lot of questions to try to find out why I had got tied up with their tour group. I gave him as few answers as I could without seeming evasive. What the Lord has spoken to me I realized would seem absolutely beyond the realm of possibility to other people. So I made no attempt to convince him of the true purpose of my trip.The Lord had sent me to meet someone in Israel, and I knew that that meeting had to take place at the Western Wall. This trip to Israel was an incredible experience. We got checked in at the airport in Tel Aviv and got on a bus that was going to take us on our first day of touring. We left New Jersey at 2:30 PM we had been in the air for 9 ½ hours. We landed at Ben Gurion airport in Tel Aviv. Our arrival in Israel was just before 7 AM. We were going to spend the first day on our tour. The sights and sounds of Israel were exciting beyond belief. I was in a land that I really belonged in. I paid close attention to everything that happened. I didn't want to miss the purpose for which I had been sent. I was sure that my meeting would have to take place at the Western Wall but the Lord had given me no directive. So it could happen almost anywhere at anytime. By the fifth day I was becoming extremely anxious. I asked the pastor several times when we were going to get to the Western Wall. On the fifth day we weremoved from our hotel on the Sea of Galilee to the Jerusalem gate Hotel in Jerusalem Israel. This was a very large hotel and had large shopping area on the bottom floor. On the first day of our tour from this location we went to Mageto. When we got back to the hotel at five o'clock that evening I was tired and my ankle hurt. I wanted to go up to my room and get cleaned up for dinner. As I approach the elevator someone grabbed my left arm from behind me. I very quickly turned around. This man appeared to be a rabbi. He bent over and asked me in an urgent tone of voice what is your name. I told him David Maendel. Then he asked me in the same urgent tone of voice what is your mother's maiden name. When I told my mother's maiden name was Wadner, he immediately said you are a Jew in the same urgent tone of voice. He also said that I should be living in Israel. I tried to ask him several questions but the man turned around and walked away. I was just beginning to get used to this. This was an extremely unusual occurrence. Nobody else on the tour group got treated this way and I never saw no one else get treated like this. This was extremely odd. After dinner I wanted to go up to my hotel room to soak my ankle in hot water. That always relieve the pain and made the swelling subsides a little. Again when I approached the elevator someone from behind me grab my right arm. I turned around very quickly. Again there was a rabbi standing behind me but not the same one. Again he asked me the same questions, what is your name again in an urgent tone of voice. And again I told him. Then he asked me what my mother's maiden name was in an extremely urgent tone of voice. Again I told him. He again stated in a tone of voice that was both urgent and somewhat surprised you are a Jew you should be living in Israel. This puzzled me greatly that had now happen twice in the same day. But I reflected back to when the Lord had told me that I was a Jew of the tribe of Judah. This encounter with two different rabbis from Israel confirmed for sure that I was a Jew. The Lord was trying to tell me something and was trying to confirm something in my spirit that I was having a very difficult time accepting.

It was on the seventh day of our tour that we finally got to go to the Western Wall. We were going to be there about 3 ½ hours. I was sure that this was going to be enough time to allow the meeting to take place that God had sent me to Israel for. At the Western Wall there's quite a large expanse of open area. I stood around at the top end of this open area for about half an hour. I was waiting for someone to come up to me and introduced him self and engage me in some form of conversation. However this never happened. So I finally walked down by the Western Wall. This was an awesome place the very tangible presence of the Lord was at that wall. I had experienced this presence at other places that we had visited. I just stood by the wall for 45 minutes or an hour with both hands on the wall and just prayed. Finally when no one approached me I asked the Lord to give me some kind of a sign if I had accomplished what she sent me to Israel for. Because at this point I had as yet not met anyone. I turned around to walk away from the wall and for the next 12 steps my right ankle completely changed. It was not healed completely. But it had changed positions.As I walked away from a wall there was a rabbi off to my right. As I got parallel to him, he turned around and stared at me with his mouth open and a look of utter astonishment on his face he stared at me for about five or six minutes. He took three or four steps towards me but then turned around and walked away. I was astonished at this response and did not want to intrude on the man if he had not approached me. It also seems to me that I was not supposed to speak to this gentleman. I walked a little farther up the gradual slope away from the wall. And just a very little way off to my right other rabbi turned around towards me and stared at me. Again he had a look of utter astonishment on his face but at the same time comprehension of what he was looking at. He was staring at me again with a look of comprehension. He stared at me like this for about six or seven minutes. He took two or three steps towards me and almost appeared to want to shake hands. But then he turned around very quickly and walked away. The two that I had met at the hotel combined with the changing position of my ankle so it did not hurt anymore confirm to me that indeed what I had been sent to Israel for had already been accomplished. I walked up to wear the pastor was standing. I told him that I was now ready to go back to America. And he said we had two more full days of the tour. He wanted to know what my hurry was. I informed him that the purpose for which I'd been sent to Israel had just been accomplished.

In March and April of 2009 I again went Israel with the same church group from Matthew West Virginia this trip was very enjoyable and very fulfilling in many ways. The difference was on this particular trip I was not on a mission for the Lord. This trip was important however because we had a different tour guide then we had the first trip. On one of the days to tour guide introduced us to her husband the husband's name was Yaeir Negev. This man was yet to play a part in my life.

Chapter 45

"I want you to go to Israel" second time

In August of 2009 I was at home on a Friday afternoon. At about three o'clock in the afternoon I was laying down. While wide-awake I entered into a vision. In the vision I was in the hallway of what I knew immediately was a large hospital. I walked down the hallway of this hospital and turned to my right and walked into a room. In this room was a man lying on a bed on his back covered with a sheet and a blanket up to his armpits his arms were on top of the blanket stretched out beside him. Beside his bed and by the head of the bed was a table or cart that was on wheels. This cart table had life support systems on it. A heart monitor, and the respirator equipment. The man on the bed was in a full coma. As I stood beside the bed looking at the man in a coma I immediately recognized him. This man was Ariel Sharon. Behind me by the wall by the door was a man about 35 years old. This man was fairly tall just less than 6 feet slender and had a white lab coat on who is a doctor. On the other side of the bed stood a young woman this woman was a nurse. On the left-hand side of the room along the wall there was a couch there was a young man standing by this couch. This young man was a little over 6 foot tall he was the son of the man lying on the bed. I walked over to where the man was laying on the bed. I told the doctor to keep a close eye on the monitors on the table especially the heart monitor. I placed my Left hand gently on the man's chest that was lying on a bed. I said to the man on the bed Mr. Sharon Jehovah God of our people Israel and Jesus the Messiah has sent me to speak with you. I said my name is David. As soon as I said my name this man became highly agitated and started moving around considerably. I gently touched his chest with my left hand and told him to please lay still. I asked him if he knew why he was in this

187

present condition. He answered me in the spirit not with his mouth. He said that he knew why he was in this present condition. That the Lord God had passed judgment on him for giving away land that belonged to Israel to the enemies of Israel to try to make peace. He also told me that he knew that this was extremely wrong. He had already repented of this and he had accepted and acknowledged Jesus as the Christ of God. And that Jesus had died on the cross and shed his blood for our sin and that he had a good knowledge Jesus Christ as his personal savior. At this point he asked me why it had taken so long for me to come to see him. He told me that two years before that when he had gotten saved and recognize Christ as his Savior that the Lord had promised to send somebody to pray for a Healing. I told him that the time and place for God's calling and purpose are not ours to determine. I said even Abraham waited 25 years for his promise to be fulfilled.

I told this man that I was going to pray for a healing to pull him out of the coma. I raised my right hand straight up above my head. My left hand was suspended above Sharon's chest about 4 inches up. I passed my hand up his chest across his face and down both sides of his head. As my hand started to pass over his chest a brilliant white light flowed down my right arm across my shoulders and down my left arminto my hand and then poured off the end of my fingers into this man's body. It was the most brilliant white ribbon of light that I had ever seen in my life. But it flowed like a slow motion stream about 6 inches wide as I pass my hand over his chest and the shoulders and above his face the light seemed to penetrate his body. As I move my hand on both sides of his head and then by the top of his head the light seemed to penetrates it. I brought my hand back over his face and the ribbon of light stopped. And I told Mr. Sharon that when I clap my hands that he was going to wake up and sit up in bed. I clap my hands sharply together and Mr. Sharon opened his eyes and sat up.

The very next morning after I had this vision I call the airlines and made arrangements to travel from Cleveland Ohio to Tel Aviv Israel. I also called the woman that had been our tour guide in March and April of 2009 and told her that I wanted to come to Israel for three weeks. She said that she would talk to Yaeir her former husband to see if I could stay with him. She got back to me within a few days and told me that arrangements had been made. She also gave me the phone number where I could reach Yaeir.

At 10 AM on 3 September 2009 I left Cleveland airport on a Continental flight to the airport in New Jersey. At 2:30 PM on that day I got onto EL/AL airplane and flew to Tel Aviv Israel. I arrived there at 7:30 AM on September 4. I was picked up at the airport by Yaeir and a friend of his who was a cab driver. He drove us to the apartment that Yaeir was living in. Yaeir had a car of his own. The next morning we made a trip to the Shaba Medical center where Ariel Sharon was being kept. For the next four or five hours we made attempts to get permission to see him. Security was apparently fairly heavy and we were not allowed in to see him. But while Yaeir was talking to the security guard and his supervisor I walked down the hallway. I was right outside of Ariel Sharon room. I started to pray that the Lord would connect me with this man. What I expected was permission to be allowed in to see Ariel Sharon in his room. The Lord did it a little differently. I actually met Arial Sharon in the spirit. And I told him that the Lord Jesus had sent me to pray for him for healing. Again he asked me the same question. Why has it taken so long for you to get here? Again I told him that our timing was not the same as God's timing. And that the Lord had only called me to do this in early August of this year. I also reaffirmed the fact that he was already saved by the blood of Jesus. He said that he was. I prayed for him for healing that the Lord would bring him out of his coma and that he would be allowed to go home to be with his family.that he would have a few months with his family before he left back into a coma and then died. This is a choice that Ariel Sharon himself had made. This part of the mission was as complete as I could make it.

While I was engaged praying for Ariel Sharon, Yaeir had met and started talking with an Arab who was a Muslim. We eventually left the Shaba Medical center and went back to Yaeir's apartment. For three or four days we did some sightseeing and some touring in Israel. Yaeir wanted me to see some of the sites that were off the normal tour routs. We also met some very interesting people. It was nice to be in a situation like this in Israel and be able to see and communicate with the local people. During the second week of my stay in Israel while driving around we stopped at the home of the

Arab that Yaeir had met at the hospital. We were invited in to this man's home. It was a beautiful home and the man was apparently quite well off. He served us espresso, fruit, and some very expensive chocolates. He spoke only Arabic. He could not speak or understand any English. And I could not speak any Arabic or Hebrew. While he was speaking with Yaeir, he asked him if I would pray for his wife. In the spirit I understood what he wanted. At first I refused. I told this Arab that he worshiped Allah. I said that I was a Christian and worship Jehovah God of our people Israel and Jesus Christ. In Arabic he said that he understood. He pointed at me and he said "you are a prophet of Jehovah, and if you pray for my wife she will be healed ". This man saw something in me that was not quite so apparent to me. I finally consented but told him that I would pray for his wife in the name of the Lord Jesus Christ and Jehovah God Israel. His wife came into the room and sat down in a chair across from me. She was walking with difficulties. I went over in front of her and knelt down on the floor. I took her hands in mine and simply prayed that the Lord Jesus Christ would bring healing to her and thanked him for the healing. I got up and went back and sat down this man's wife got up and walked out of the room completely healed. What a powerful statement in an Arab community about the power and authority of the Lord Jesus Christ. Something had happened to me when I got off the airplane in Israel on September 4. As soon as I got off the airplane in Israel the glory of God had settled down on me. What people saw in me was that glory. The glory of God has not been seen in Israel for over 2000 years. That is why I was such a strange sight at the time. It was a few days later when we went to Jerusalem. We spent about half a day there. We had just left Jerusalem at about 6 PM when Yaeir got a phone call from a friend that he hadn't seen in 15 years. The man invited us over to his home. The directions they gave us required us to make a left turn immediately to get to his home. We were quite close. When we got to these people's home we were escorted into the house and into the living room. Yaeir and his friend went around on the left side of the table and sat down and started talking. This man could speak very little English. His wife came over in front of me as soon as I came into the house. She grabbed my arms above the elbows with both of her hands. She was quite strong and squeezed my arms fairly hard. She could also speak fluent English. She said in a very emotional tone of voice, "you are a prophet of God you have to pray for my sister". She repeated this several times. I assured her that we would pray for her sister before we left that evening. And I pried her hands off my arms. I tried to go and sit down. She again got in front of me and grabbed my arms. This time she started shaking me. She said "you don't understand my sister has lymphoma. You are a prophet of God you have to pray for my sister because when you pray for my sister she will be completely healed". Now she was on the verge of tears. I told her I am not trying to put you off but we will pray for you sister tonight. The two men talked until midnight. I stopped them talking and told them that we had to pray for the man sister-in-law. We held hands around the table and started to pray. I pray for a total healing for this lady whom I had never met. About halfway through the prayer the Lord stopped me he said "I want you to stop praying and I want you to tell this woman that her sister has been totally healed. But tell her that for the next couple of months she has to go to doctors to verify her healing". This news was extremely well received.What an awesome few days we had already spent in Israel. The Lord Jesus had shown up and a powerful and magnificent way. In just these two encounters of healing he touched lives. The Lord also made a powerful witness of his presence in Israel. On the day that the Arab woman was healed we wanted to attend the funeral of a young Israeli pilot that had died in an F-16 crash. We drove to where the funeral was being held in a cemetery. We got as close to the podium as we possibly could. All of the top government leaders of Israel were at this funeral. All of the top military brass was also at this funeral. In fact they were almost 10,000 people at his funeral. This in itself was an amazing sight. While his funeral was going on we were just a few steps away from the top military and government leaders. I also discovered by looking around there was not a single dry eye at this event. The entire nation of Israel seem to be mourning this young pilot's death.

The glory of God that had settled on me when I was in Israel stayed with me for two weeks after I got home. I have been under a powerful anointing in my life on many occasions. But this was the first experience I had being under the glory of God. When a powerful anointing lifts you feel like you have been abandoned. When the glory of God lifted I felt like I'd been thrown in the garbage heap. I felt utterly abandoned by God. I was totally unsure whether I had accomplished what I was supposed to in Israel are not. What a powerful statement was made for the presence of Jesus the Messiah and his powerful ability to heal but also to touch lives and affect change in people. I did not feel quite right about my encounter with Ariel Sharon. I did not feel as though I had completed that part of my mission.

Chapter 46

Prophetic Confirmation

It was in the second week of October of 2009 that a prophet from the southern part of the United States came to a local church in Alliance Ohio. He was to speak at this church Sunday night Monday night and Tuesday night. I really did not want to go to see this man. But I felt urging by the Holy Spirit to be at these meetings. I sat in the third pew back from the front. This man's name was Dr. Jordan. When Dr. Jordan came in he went up behind the large pulpit on the platform. He was apparently uncomfortable so he grabbed a smaller pulpit that was standing on the platform and brought it down to floor level in front of all the pews. He set up almost directly in front of where I was sitting. He arranged a few papers on the pulpit and then looked up. When he looked up he made eye contact with me. He just stared at me for about three or four minutes I also held his gaze. This profit saw the very presence of God in me. He caught himself and started preaching. The service that night lasted until 9:30 PM. Monday night I came back to that church again. I was absolutely sure that this man had a word from the Lord for me personally. I felt that it was important enough that I stayed here and try to find out what it was. Monday night service ended at about 10:00 PM. But this prophet of God never called me out. I came back again on Tuesday night because I was convinced that my presence at this service was important. By 8:00 PM this man had not yet called me out. I decided it was time to leave. Dr. Jordan was in the middle of preaching and I did not think he would notice me going out. I picked up my coat and got my Bible and my hat but had not moved yet. Dr. Jordan stopped preaching and said that there was somebody that was getting ready to leave. And he asked that that person that was getting ready to leave please stay. He said that the Lord had given him a powerful word for that person. I was absolutely sure that Dr. S Jordan had not seen me getting ready to leave he had never looked in my direction.At 8:50 PM this prophet of God came up the aisle and stopped just at the end of my pew. He was looking at the rest of the congregation. He said that when the children of Israel were called out of Egypt and they first saw the glory of God they did not know what to call it.They called it the Shekinah Glory of God. By this time I was already standing up because I knew he was going to call me out. He looked at me and he called me down to the front of the church. He told me that when I was in Israel that the glory of God was on me. I had never talk to this man before so he could not have found out from me that I was in Israel. This prophet of God was giving me a message from the Lord. He also said that I had become quite discouraged since I came back from Israel. He told me that when the glory of God lifts that it makes a man feel that way. He also knew that I was looking for a powerful word from the Lord of what I was supposed to do next. And he told me that he knew a lot more,but that he could not tell me because he was not permitted. Thatwhen I was sent back to Israel I would again be under the powerful presence of the glory of God. And that the Lord Jesus himself would tell me what he wanted me to do. That the Lord Jesus would be with me every step of the way.This answered a lot of questions for me. One thing that I have never had an abundance of is a patients. It has taken the Lord 63 ½ years out of my 64 years of life to try to teach me to patiently wait until he moves. On so many different occasions if something has not happened immediately or soon, I have had a tendency to cause it to happen on my own. The problem with that policy is it always takes the Lord time afterwards to straighten out the mess that I made. I have to learn to wait on God. If God doesn't send me than the time must not be right. But I think by now the Lord has the upper hand and I have learned through the university of hard knocks to wait.

I still had considerable doubt about Israel and my trip of September2009. I did not actually see a manifestation of what I was sent to Israel to accomplish. And the thought kept crossing my mind was I aggressive enough in pursuit of the purpose that God sent me for. Did I really try hard enough to overcome obstacles?

This question continued to plague me and never completely left my mind or my spirit. For a long while I was still a little bit uneasy about this. I think that the Lord allows us times to go through periods like this and to reflect and meditate on what he asked us to do and what was actually accomplished.

In April of 2010 I went to work for a local auto parts store delivering parts to repair shops. I enjoyed this job but found out that because of my right leg I could only work five hours a day. This was far better than sitting at home with not much to do. My knee was starting to give me trouble and my ankle also hurt quite a bit of the time. This job for the local auto parts store lasted until the end of 2010. In September 2010 just one year after I got back from Israel the Lord answered my prayer with the typical sign similar to the one he had showed me at the Western Wall in 2007.On September 22 of that year at about 9:00 AM the Lord started to rebuild my right knee. The tendons and ligaments that had been torn out of my knee in a motorcycle accident on March 30, 2007 were completely restored from 9:00 AM on the 22nd till about 7:00 PM on 23 September. Each time tendon or ligament would stretch across my knee and reattach itself I could feel it. This process of reconstructing my knee was amazing to experience. To be able to feel each tendon or ligament being replaced was more fun than being wide awake during major surgery and not have to experience pain. This also told me without a shadow of doubt that what I had been sent to Israel for in 2009 was fully accomplished. It is so wonderful when our heavenly father lets us know that we were obedient and did what we are sent to do. And it's not that it puts a gold star at the top of our paper but just gives us the peace of mind that all is well. God's grace and mercy far exceeds our greatest expectations.

Chapter 47

The Lord Prepared Me For This

The Lord is working out the details for the rest of the mission that I have to complete before I'm allowed to go home to be with the Lord himself in heaven. I desire more than anything else in the world to see my God the Lord Jesus face-to-face. To be able to see again the prints of the nails in His hands and in his feet. On three different occasions in my life I have seen the Lord Jesus face to face. On four different occasions I have been in heaven in the spirit. The mission for witch I have been prepared for since the moment I was conceived I am almost ready to accomplish. This book cannot really be completed until that mission is finished. But that mission will kill me. This book will have to stay at the point it is at now untill we enter into eternity. It is difficult to know just how to close a book when there's still so much that should be a part of this that cannot yet be written.

This book tells the story of God Almighty raising up a prophet from very humble beginnings for special work. I have never in the past or in the present seen myself able to accomplish the work that the Lord Jesus is preparing me for. There does however, arrive a time when the Lord personally calls us to service that we recognize that service, acknowledge it, and receive it in our mind and spirit. I am not the type to declare myself to a lot of people. I do not use this opportunity for that purpose. I merely state this purpose for the glory of God. I state this purpose also that people might understand at what point we are in prophetic history.In December 2004 I was sitting on my bed reading a magazine about two profits who will prophesy in Israel for 3 ½years. The Lord spoke to me and said "this is what I am preparing you for to be one of these two men". I do not debate this or argue it. I do not try in any way shape or form to justify it. I did not apply for the job. I did not seek the Lord for special treatment or recognition. As a matter of fact I fought the Lord for six months after He informed me of His purpose for me. As I stated earlier in this book the Lord's answer to me came very harshly. I have also been verified by people that the Lord has sent to me and prophesied to me that they know what the Lord is preparing me for. On six different occasions since 2005 this has occurred. In the mouth of two or three witnesses the word of God is confirmed. I accept what the Lord has spoken to me and make every effort to be totally obedient to the Lord. It must also be understood that what the Lord is preparing me for I cannot do anyway. The work for which I have been prepared can only be done by the power of the Holy Spirit working through me. This humble profit has no abilities in himself to even begin to understand how these things must come to pass. I do not brag in this book on myself. All my boasts is in my God.

The Lord Jesus has been so incredibly gracious and merciful in my life and in the lives of my two children that I cannot justifiably give him enough credit in a simple manuscript such as this. If we learn to believe in what the Lord is doing, and in what the Lord has promised us, and also have faith in the Lord then He will accomplish all things promised until we all make our crossing to the other side and are able to stand in His presence and commune with Him face-to-face. I am satisfied at this point that my life has been for the large part lived to the glory of God. I have given myself totally and wholeheartedly and completely to the work of my God. I hold no reserve back for myself. I make no contingency that if the Lord should tarry that I will do such and such or go here or there. There are things that I would like to do and places that I would like to see in this world. But I will have all of eternity to do that. The most important thing in my life at this point is to be totally obedient to the Lord Jesus when He moves me by the power of the Holy Spirit to do a work that He has prepared me for. I have declared myself a bondservant of the Lord Jesus. My aim and intent is that everything I do, or should I say everything that the Holy Spirit accomplishes through me is done to the glory of God. My prayer is continually that when I am seen by anyone that they actually see the presence of the Holy Spirit in me and the presence of the Shekinah glory of

God around me and glorify and praise the God of my fathers. I also pray that this book and the things that are written in it will be a powerful witness for what God has already accomplish through this humble prophet. And that those that have declared themselves by the works that they do the enemies of God may yet have an opportunity to turn from their wrong ways and give God glory and honor and praise and worship Him as they should. But let it be known without any doubt that those that refuse to honor God for who and what He is and refuse to recognize the Lord Jesus as the Christ of God, the only begotten son of God who died on the cross and shed His blood that the sin of the world through Him might be wiped out, will be judged. But those who refuse to believe will eventually be judged by God Almighty.